Praise for *Holy Here Wholy You*

"An embodied intuitive and gifted teacher, Kim Lincoln is a skilled naviga-
tor of the subtle landscape of the soul and the intricate labyrinth of 'ordi-
nary reality.' Through her own profound journey into these two hemispheres
of her being, spanning several decades, she has discovered—and is able to
articulate—often overlooked nuances, which are not always easy to detect.

In Holy Here Wholly You, *Kim has uniquely interwoven ancient and*
contemporary modalities and created a valuable guidebook for anyone in-
terested in deepening their connection with themselves and inhabiting a uni-
fied field. Like the ancient Sumerian Goddess, Inanna, who descended into
and returned from the underworld rejuvenated and restored, Kim has re-
turned from many years of inner exploration as a wise elder—well equipped
to assist others. In her willingness and capacity to meet all of herself, she is
now a way shower with bountiful offerings, holding a bright wisdom lamp."
—**Rashani Réa**, author of *Beyond Brokenness* and founder of Kipuka-
maluhia Sanctuary, www.rashani.com

"In language that is both grounded and lyrical, Kim Lincoln describes with
a rare kind of eloquence the work of the soul, the embodiment of our divine
nature. She combines scholarship, science and a lifetime of experience to of-
fer a practice in which body, mind and emotion are integrated into whole-
ness, opening us to live authentically and consciously, to be who we really
are: spiritual beings in a physical world."
—**Linda Strever,** author of *Don't Look Away*, www.LindaStrever.com

"Kim writes an expansive mapping of the human's evolutionary journey
from unconscious trances, through layers of mistaken identity, and into the
realms of spiritual integration. What Jung refers to as the Sacred Marriage,

Kim details in her mind, body and emotional skills to create integrated healing, providing the foundation and space for true spiritual integration."
—**Deborah Dooley, PhD,** author of *Journeying Into Wholeness With Map and Skills,* evolutionary astrology psychotherapist

"*This book has emerged in its own perfect time as we witness humanity's awakening and our planetary evolution. It provides a clear pathway to uncover our own sacred wisdom and our soul's true, infinite nature. Discover the stories of our ancient lineages, play with the dynamic processes, and in the space between words, feel the tender transmission of love, calling us home to the shining Ones that we are.*"
—**Diane Sonntag, LMP, LcE**, devotional musician and harpist, www.HolyOlyGirls.com, alchemist esthetician, Practice Presencing Seminars, www.Presence.abmp.com

"*The nature of 'the work' that Ms. Lincoln supports is the journey all souls take to individuation. Her approach grounds inquiry about the progress of the soul in the body and in the here and now. Ms. Lincoln refers to the soul as having a terrain, one that is unique to each person. Just as a mountain can be scaled from numerous approaches, an individual can navigate his or her own terrain from almost any starting point. Her tools empower people to work with the content of their own lives to grow and realign with naturally given beauty and essence through a process of integration and acceptance. The process is so elegantly simple and yet yields quiet miracle after miracle among her students.*"
—**Mary Beth Brown,** health system transformation specialist and rowing coach

"*A spiritual map for internal insight. The content is brilliant, a map to the soul for those willing to take the adventure. Following the thread of truth to what is essential provides a guideline to support emotional and physical rebalance from trauma. This book lays the groundwork for understanding and trust of our inherent systems to pick up the thread.*

It has been tremendously successful in helping me walk through the dreadful shattering, spinning loss from trauma, through to hope, curiosity, then rediscovery of a wellspring of resources to heal. A body of work that has provided substantial insight to guide child, adolescent and adult patients in their internal process toward recovery following traumatic injury."
––Terri-Lynn Cousley, MS, CCC-SLP, specialist in acquired and developmental neurogenic disorders

"Kim's extraordinary, subtle awareness is a gentle guide to the inner light of the soul. Her pioneering work in navigating the inner landscapes builds on the ancient wisdom teaching to "know thyself." It also brings new dimensions in perceiving and realizing what we might become.

I am deeply grateful for Kim's impeccable terrain of essence work. How precious this learning to integrate the divine feminine and masculine and to feel the body harmonize with the inner work, knowing that we are continuous with both Earth and Cosmos.

Tracking the inner landscapes requires an adept intuitive, yet to write about it is a true work of love."
––Barbara M. V. Scott, MS, wildlife biologist, sacred agriculture practitioner, and light root researcher

"Kim masterfully transmits Essential Nature, actualizing a portal for embodied Self- Awareness."
––Dr. Jessica Rose, DC, Embodied Brilliance, co-founder and facilitator of the School of Awakening to Wholeness

"Kim Lincoln's keen perceptual abilities reveal hidden psychological trauma embedded within the nervous system. Kim is adept at taking students through a 'depth' process to access the state of wholeness that is already present, but hidden or obscured behind afflicted emotions, stories, and unconscious patterns. This is true freedom, the freedom to be who they really are in all their aliveness, vitality and fullness, being able to access the living and loving heart many have been cut off from. Holy Here Wholly You *is a book that will change your life."*

––**Naomi Lombardi, MA**, clinical psychologist, author of *Dancing in the Underworld: The Quest for Wholeness,* workshop presenter of "Riding the Wind: Breaking Free of the Shackles of Trauma"

"Kim Lincoln's expression of this work is truly trans-formative. My work as an acupuncturist has changed radically from a fix problems mentality to supporting the whole being of the individual. This shift has radically altered my personal life as well by helping me to accept parts of myself that previously I was in strain with. Her writings are foundation building blocks that I cannot recommend more highly. They are at the root of the school I have co-founded, my professional work, and my approach to life. Thank you Kim."

––**Brent Swift, LAc,** co-founder and facilitator of the School of Awakening to Wholeness

"Kim Lincoln's radiant weave of ancient wisdom teachings, current science, and open-hearted vulnerability presents a coherent pathway into the direct experience of our true, essential Self.

In the plethora of offerings available for self-exploration and consciousness development, Kim's work is truly extraordinary in its depth and ability to bring us through our entanglements of long-held beliefs and emotional

turmoil into the ability to access our soul's essence. We have the opportunity in this work to engage consciously with the subtle energy of the soul - the Beloved."
—**Jordan Taylor,** student

"I am thrilled and inspired to see Kim's lifelong work become available to us all!! This is a beautiful tapestry of wisdom, weaving ancient mystic texts with the insight and clarity of Kim's life work as a spiritual teacher. It is an honor to call her teacher and friend and fellow dancer in the light."
—**Karen Feeley, DC,** Whole Being Olympia

"As a teacher of Kundalini yoga, I have a connection to Kim Lincoln's teachings that have permeated the lens from which I see. It's an understanding that we are enough–– in fact, we are brilliant beyond measure.

Kim taught me how to guide people into traveling that mysterious territory of soul essence through sensing their own body. After all these years, I am still amazed at the accessibility of these presencing sessions. This work offers a bridge to understanding one's true self. I am eternally grateful to Kim for sharing these simple yet powerful tools and teachings with the world."
—**Jessica Ryan**, founder of the Shakti Sanctuary

"Because of this work, I have been able to slowly feel my anger and my power and realize that anger isn't bad. Instead of rage and violence, this energy can be channeled in different ways––to feel strength and establish boundaries, which is something I was never able to do and now I get daily practice (ha!). This learning has been such a blessing for me."
—**Caitlin Richards,** student

HOLY HERE WHOLY YOU

Discovering Your Authentic Self

Kim Lincoln

WHITE LION  Olympia, Washington

Holy Here Wholy You: Discovering Your Authentic Self

Author: Kim Lincoln

Editor: Ann West

Cover Design: Carolyn Reynolds, graphics and layout, Buck Art, www.buckart.net, "artist of genuine simulated Paleolithic Cave Art."

Cover Art: Original painting by artist Jennifer Johnson. Jennifer practices creative arts and awareness of energies. Her pieces include paintings, drawings, poetry, video, and a few songs. In her works, she expresses subtle qualities, feelings, and flows she witnesses in nature and inner landscapes. www.jentiful.com

Title Page Illustration: "Embodied Cosmic Human" by Kim Lincoln

Back Cover Head Shot Photo: Sandy Scribner

Library of Congress Control Number: 2017900194
CreateSpace Independent Publishing Platform
North Charleston, South Carolina

First published in 2017 by
White Lion Publishing, LLC
6227 Northill Dr. SW
Olympia, WA 98512

ISBN – 13: 9781542374934
ISBN – 10: 1542374936

Self-Transformation/ Spirituality

The views offered here are the sole opinions of the author. They are in no way a substitute for sound medical advice, nor are they intended to prescribe. All matters regarding your health require medical or psychological supervision. Neither the author nor the publisher shall be liable or responsible for any loss or damage allegedly arising from any information or suggestion made in this book. The author is held harmless against any unintended encroachment upon another author's opinion. Any part that is known to belong to another has been documented here. Certain words such as *presencing* are those of the author's own work and her teacher's work and not necessarily comparable to current usage in American English. The English language offers very few words to describe the nature of this work, and so terms used here may sound like, but not necessarily mean the same thing as, the use of such words in other contexts.

In full gratitude and appreciation of my students
for their genuine dedication.
This book is for you.

Acknowledgments

It takes a community ~ In boundless gratitude, thank you, thank you, thank you! Without my students' persistence, this book may not have happened. I believe you know who you are!

To my editor, Ann West, how did I get to be so blessed? I realize I have challenged every notion of writing etiquette. Yet your kindness to take me under your wing has been an unfathomable blessing. I have great admiration and honor for your precision and wisdom as master diamond cutter, finely chiseling away what is not needed to reveal with clarity what lies below. You have gone far beyond the call of duty, encouraging me not to give up.

Dear Barbara M. V. Scott, biodynamic compost master, you appeared out of the blue. Recognizing raw material, you gently yet persuasively planted me within Ann's view. Thank you for our introduction and candid reflection upon what I would need in order to bloom this project. You are an angel.

I wish to thank my advisers and tech team. You rock! Each one has stepped forward at just the right time. Tarik Muqaddam, Geri Baldwin, Jennifer Johnson, Angela Francois, and Linda Strever, your research, documentation, and motivation saved the day.

I've loved witnessing the metamorphosis of the book cover's vibrant original art (painted by Jennifer Johnson) in the hands of my graphic artist, Carolyn Reynolds, queen of patience. Staying true to this body of teaching, where two or more gather in the mystery of Love, she has brought forth a new form. Thank you for birthing this joined creative expression.

My love and appreciation for the many collogues and students whose poetry, quotes, and testimonials have graced these pages. The loving support of this project and your own testaments shine through with your brilliance.

A bounty of thanks to dear readers who helped fine-comb the manuscript and provided editorial comments. Thank you, Hazel Gilley, Shannon Baker, Martha McMahon, Mary Beth Brown, Diane Sonntag, Naomi Lombardi, Jordan Taylor, Sydne Cogburn, Erica Conner, Thomas Serra, and Alan Gutman for your spunky delight and bright feedback!

To all, too many to name, who responded to my campaign to fund this project, wow! I received nearly double what I had asked! I can't thank you enough for your tremendous outpouring of support and engagement with this endeavor. And a big hug to those who spearheaded the workshops: Will Vaninwagen, Karen Feeley, Michelle Morris, Hazel Gilley, Jennifer Johnson, Phillip Miller, and all the wonderful attendees joined in Pamela Favro's gorgeous Dancing Cedars Retreat Center! And to all the folks at Kickstarter and CreateSpace who have made it possible for folks like me to share our work, thank you!

Were it not for you – Fran Kersch, Joanne Cooper, and Erica Conner––pressing me to share my work, I may have still been hiding out in my little room at Fusion. Oh that wondrous, fateful day when you asked and said yes. We've come a long way!

Terri-Lynn and Ed Cousley, Diane Bloom, Sharon Lincoln, Diane Sonntag, Jessica Rose, Brent Swift, Heather Flournoy, Mary Beth Brown, Jessica Ryan, and Rosie Finn – you held my feet to fire and fanned the flames. Thank you for your unrelenting faith in me.

Joan Kenley and Joan Spangler, you lit the flame and initiated a movement that would have a positive lifelong impact because of your astute expertise and goodwill – I can't thank you enough.

My body and being gratefully sing praises to the loving and expert hands of Dr. Dan Gleeson, Dr. Jessica Rose, Brent Swift, and Diane Sonntag who provided me with a nourishing wellspring of rejuvenation and regeneration in support of the monumental pace that the river of Grace issued forth while maintaining my fulltime private practice and simultaneously writing this book during the last a year and a half!

And last but not least, I acknowledge four pillars, a foundation upon which my life has been built. You have shaped my many ways and of you I blossom with your finest attributes. First, Carol Jean, dear Mom, please know I am living the life you dreamt. Our 4:00 a.m. meetings when I was a child taught me of the complex trauma of your life and its effect. With appreciation, I embrace the confidentiality of your secrets and the ways you've entrusted and cultured my intuitive self.

Bob Lincoln (Dad, I call you), with love I thank you for your self-lessness and genuine support. Who knows where I may have wandered had you not entered my life. You tethered me to reality, creating unwavering stability. It took me years to recognize you have always been here and to trust the truth of that.

Faisal Muqaddam, blessings for your great love and lifetimes shared. Your mastery of inquiry in navigating the terrain of essence helped me to cherish and reclaim my authentic self. Had not our serendipitous encounter occurred, I might not be alive today. For you I have immense gratitude.

And to my mentor, mischief-maker in delight, and dear friend Alan Gutman, dancer in the spheres of light, your brilliance of genius is unmatchable in thinking outside of the box! You are treasured.

To my teachers seen and unseen, your wisdom has paved my way. For all of you, my inner guidance, and the Great Source of All, I am truly thankful. Of One Mind and One Heart, may everyone someday come to Know this sacred Blessing ~ Love.

Contents

Introduction

Embodied Intuition

It is my greatest joy teaching others how to access, recognize, and directly experience their divine essence. Through my workshops and classes, I've had the honor to witness extraordinary transformations, welcoming ways of showing up to participate fully in daily life as a spiritual light being in this physical world. I wish to thank my students for their persistence in asking me to write down some of what I've taught in class. This book is not only a helpful review but also a valuable tool for anyone wishing to deepen their connection with themselves. It serves as a fundamental orientation to the bigger picture in the area of self-growth and wellness, integrating many modalities. As a guidebook, it is a helpful support for learning about the mind-body-soul connection and what it is to be a consciously embodied human being.

Here I offer some of the basic tools needed to create positive change in your life. I share some simple exercises to help bridge the conscious and unconscious as well as introduce the three centers: the mental, emotional, and physical. These exercises arose out of my own need many years ago. As I opened to new levels of consciousness, the expansiveness of my spiritual practice freaked out the body, the bodywork triggered my mind, and my mind played hide and seek, setting off emotional upheavals. And 'round and 'round it went. It was crazy making. I wasn't finding a modality that held all these pieces together in a way that I could successfully return to balance and function in the world.

When a spiritual master told me that I was perfect and whole, the ego took off and ran with an inflated feeling of being special and better than. As a result, this separation created a hole, and then the ego deflated, identified with the deficiency of an unconscious pattern laid down long ago. My personality was swinging from the highest of the high to the lowest of the low with not much in between. I needed something simple that could help me bridge the gap and connect with my wholeness wherever I was, whenever I could. I sought a way that would create constant contact with all parts of the whole and be a reliable re-Source. When I developed these simple exercises for my own growth and practiced them, my life began to change––I mean, really change for the better. And I began experiencing more constancy and ease as a result.

If you or someone you know is highly sensitive to the impressions of others, is empathic and merges with suffering, or has experienced a lot of trauma, then reading these pages may be useful. The chapters explore some of the ways in which we distort or embody truth, trust, love, and our divine nature through the lens of the personal "I," the personality of our egoistic identity. You will discover what that mechanism is really about and learn ways of reclaiming what is essentially true. You will also learn to discern the energetic movement to which we unconsciously give ourselves, turning us either away from or toward life. With this knowledge, we come to trust our intuition and make consciously informed choices, which instantaneously returns us to the wholeness of our authentic self.

This book is the first in a series of three complementary volumes that focus on orientation, application, and actualization principles, the culmination of my life's work. Here I share my personal process and the history of this work, as well as offer practical guidance to transform complicated concepts into simple solutions. May these pages prove useful in your life and benefit you in every way.

We Are Whole, We Are Sacred

I f you are reading this, you are ready to explore consciousness. You have responded to a particular resonance, a kind of knowing, even if you are not aware that you know. The Knowing Self is in relationship with the ego, both its innocent and its wise aspects. This book explores a number of themes set against the backdrop of such intricate connections. To explore the complexity of personal development, I use examples from my own history, giving you glimpses of how unconscious patterns can affect one's life. I also share what helped me to make new choices, writing it out so that you too can learn to feel more connected and whole.

The first half of the book explores two primary types of knowing. Initially, we meet the knowing that doesn't know that it knows. This shows up as all sorts of defensive tactics that get in the way of one's underlying truth. Such behavior includes the autopilot of habit and the pain of our human condition. We don't yet know that who we are is sacred and whole.

Next is a knowing that knows that it doesn't know. Our consciousness is awakening. By being responsible for our miscreations, we thus teach the lesser-developed self it is now safe to come forward and grow up. Maturation is an integrative process in which we recognize what we are doing and the clever ways we encourage a false separation from being. We learn to spot any efforts involved in maintaining such separation. Here we practice the art of surrender on a continuum that involves falling and then dissolving to assimilate a new form.

This brings us to the later portion of the book——self-realization, a direct experience of knowing. In the awakening process, the knower who knows is completely surrendered to the wisdom of undoing and, in return, receives guidance from such living grace. Here one discovers that enlightenment is nothing more than being in-light-in-the-moment. The knower trusts the fluid movement of being, neither resisting nor exaggerating the uniqueness of an authentic self.

Existing in faultless movement, however, requires time and patience to develop one's capacity to be here. We may meet resistance due to our instinctual self, which resides in the unconscious underworld of the cells. The catch is that self-actualization cannot occur unless we can drop into the body. Only in this way can we avoid splitting off parts from our entirety. Physicality helps us feel the embodied wholeness of both formless and form living in a holistic way. This is a double-edged sword because whenever the nervous system lets go and involuntary movement arises in the flow of being, fear and grasping also may arise. Therefore, the chapters discuss a series of responses one can use to balance out the body again.

On the topic of wholeness, the biggest question I had was where to begin. If at the heart of wholeness there is essentially love, is love enough? That depends on what you call love. In my case, the open lid to Pandora's box revealed a body of pain. This is where I decided to step in. Pain is the most charged stage of our journey. It is where we often get stuck, not knowing a different way. We see that what we have been doing no longer works, and now——through love——we need to change and release the pain.

So why is change so important yet so difficult? In writing this book, I wanted to share what in my own practice and the practice of my students made a difference in allowing for positive change. While discerning between genuine love and its masked imitation, I learned that behind every virtuous quality of love lies an insidious aspect of fear. As an exemplar for your own journey, I invite you to travel with us, the many voices arising from my own fear.

On the road to wholeness, I was required to face repression and the recovered memories of forgotten experiences. These had driven away the power of my vehicle as I mistakenly separated from the reality of being here now in search of the Light far away. To heal, I began to embrace the self-realization that it was only the "me" of my limited patterns who had gone, for the Light is always at hand——indeed, my very existence.

Each one of us is the brightly burning light of our original expression. Yet I, like many others, was seeking outward confirmation. What I learned was that self-realization requires turning within to re-inhabit our beautiful mortal body. For hidden within lies the terrain of a mysterious language pointing the way. From out of the convoluted universe of my personal experience arose a precise map, returning me home to the safe and hospitable refuge of my authentic self——the wholeness of my soul.

Throughout the following chapters, I have provided a condensed overview of the egoistic, energetic, and esoteric landscape of the mind, body, and soul. As you embrace powerful yet barely perceivable integral truths, you will further deepen access to your true self. Presence and inquiry become key when tracking each thought, sensation, and emotion. In addition to giving priceless examples from my students, I point out pitfalls you may encounter if your witnessing capacity is not yet developed. I also offer skillful ways to navigate the unconscious momentum and tricky edge between what is known and unknown to support the growth of self-knowing.

The knowledge that the unconscious self lives buried in the body is not new. Yet during this recent century and the advent of neuroscience, what once was cloaked in the secret teachings of the Mystery Schools has been made available to more than a chosen few. More and more people are realizing that the way of domination and repression is not working. The process of encircling a larger humanity asks that we individually step up to the challenge of supporting the whole. Change begins with us exposing any ways that we are self-inflicting separation. We cannot teach what we do not intrinsically know, for we bring to the equation where we are or are not willing to go. This true knowing arises from repeated practice and direct embodied experience of heaven and earth, integrating ego and essence while promoting our ability to be humanly whole. May this book inspire the remembrance of and unity with the wisdom teacher within so that we all may thrive and grow!

Inshalla,

In Love, Light, and Peace. So Be It.

Kim Lincoln

Orientation and History

When God's abundance flooded existence
I was fashioned.
And since the earliest of time
I was bestowed upon the teachings of Love,
Then from the ingredients of my heart
God moulded the key to the treasure of meaning.

Ah. Love could thou and I with Fate conspire
To group the sorry Scheme of Things entire!
Would not we shatter it to bits——and then
Re-mould it nearer to the Heart's Desire!

—— Omar Khayyam, *Rubaiyat*[1]

Chapter 1

The Essence of Love

From magical beginnings to the dark night of the soul, our journey is a collision of the terrible and the beautiful forged into one. It is only when we can embrace the terrible without judgment that our full richness of being can come through in ways mysterious as we perceive this larger view.[2] This book is a simple offering to help us discern, embody, and cherish both our human experience and the terrain of our essence, the subtle energy body of soul.

We will explore the intimate relationship of this dance as well as the resulting confusion among different aspects of the mind of beliefs, the body of instincts, and the motion of emotions. As we experience how our beliefs and emotions affect the body, we can apply simple practices to help us return to balance and reconnect with our true nature. Without distortion, we can realize the encoded virtuous aspects of our being that we once confused with mundane reality. May this work help to light the way, sparking the brilliance of your life's purpose and inspiring the emergence of your fullest potential.

Mine has been a fierce and narrow path, both a blessing and a curse depending upon one's view. At certain times, I have had to rely solely upon my own soul's force, because any deviation would have caused debilitating repercussions. Yet in the long run, the building up and tearing down of reliance upon anything false has expanded my capacity to listen to and trust, without a doubt, my inner guidance. It is from this gauge that I share what has innately arisen and oriented me toward a higher truth.

The simplicity of the exercises I offer arose from the guidance of my consciousness many years ago, showing how we can make real our dreams and bring down to earth our imagination. We thus can usher into physical form the seeds of imaginal conception, contrary to how we think things *should* be done. Yes, you will be unlearning what you think reality is about.

Longing for Home

Within each of us, there is a longing, a yearning in search of a place we can call home——a home of our choosing, free from familiar entanglements. This is a place that nurtures us, where we can fully rest and be sustained, trusting and receiving deep medicine to heal the wounds of our past. Here we will unveil a territory that regenerates and renews our sense of purpose, a terrain where we can thrive. The burning desire to be true to ourselves can launch us on journeys across continents or from one relationship or job to another in search of "just right." Maybe we'll have a baby to cure our dilemma or buy more stuff to satisfy this hunger, or even become a star. But what happens when the partner leaves, we don't have the child, our career falls apart, or throngs of admirers take up with others?

It is thus that our real work begins, a work that can truly support our essential Self. A new perspective shows us how not to become swallowed up in the false, limited sense of identification that is reflected by our resistance and reactivity. We begin to overcome a past in which we attempted to camouflage certain traumas and loss by creating such ineffective distractions, which we imagined would protect us from our fear of feeling fully alive.

At this point, we face the emptiness of our separation, the existential loneliness of our self-imposed isolation, exposing our hole of unquenchable deficiency that no object can fill.[2] In laying down our pride, and through willingness to meet and be with unfathomable pain, we begin to access the potentialities of our true nature. This is the where the incessant drive "to get" ceases as we rest in the full abundance of Being.

It is only then that we can recognize how the pain of separation is caused by our own unconscious choices, which are driven by the conditioned patterns of our past. And once realized, we shall truly flourish; for we've gone from there to here, and here is home. Our painful alienation and isolation are nothing more than our own lack of connection with True Essence, resulting in the haunting, lonely void of a vacuous identity. From this hole of deficiency, even when in a room surrounded by others, we will feel the depth of the falseness, aloneness, and the alienation of that limitation. And so, by putting down our victimization, righteousness, regression, and prejudice, we let go and surrender. Thereafter, we receive the blessings of what is essentially true, healing the wounding of our perceived lack to claim what we have always intrinsically known. This "knowing" appears to each of us as our own unique way.[3] As I share throughout this book how it came about for me, I invite you to notice ways that the hints of self-knowing began for you.

Trusting the Radiance of Grace

As a three-year-old, I perceived the radiant presence of two white lions––great beings of translucent light, appearing and then slipping away seamlessly through shafts of sunbeams across my playroom floor. I also witnessed apparitions of those who had passed away and beheld other visitations in luminescent form. Thus, I learned early on to trust my subtle perceptions and the unconditional plenitude of benevolent Grace. By the age of six, I knew in my marrow that I would teach, yet the feeling I had didn't match the model of the surrounding world view. So after many decades of exploring this and that and of trying on different hats, I eventually arrived at an edge where my choices were either to stay frozen before a boundless drop into the abyss, holding tight to the last vestiges of a false identity, or to surrender my self-limitation and fall into the absorption of the Great Unknown. I chose the latter and discovered the guidance of a vast, intimate quietude, blessed by an all-embracing, expansive buoyancy of depth, grace, and plentitude

To this day, each moment is a treasure-filled surprise that nourishes every fiber of my being. I bring to you decades of weaving energetic science and ancient mysticism into a simple, direct way of accessing one's true nature. I am dedicated to teaching how to connect with the healer within––your inner guru. On this path of freedom, you can empower your choices, magnify discernment, and embrace your magnificence. By accepting the bountiful radiance of the being you are, you in turn show appreciation for Creator's gift––the existence that you've been granted. It is an ultimate action of love to be all we can be, to be aligned with our innate truth, and to step out into the world from here. And so now, let's begin...

Vast is this limitless brilliance...a sonorous brightness, as far as sight can reach. Light upon light... I am the light... I am consciousness.

Below... a portal opens, I watch... Suddenly... pulling... pulling... pulled... down....

I am conceived.

From my earliest memories, I wanted to know: Why am I here, and what is my purpose? Who am I? Who is this *I*? One day while playing a spelling game, the secret word I hid from my class was *ego*. And when the letters were laid out across the chalkboard, my teacher declared that a child of seven couldn't possibly know the word or its meaning. Therefore, my offering was invalid. But it wasn't so. Hadn't my mother intimately shared its meaning with me from early on. I was her confidant and understood well the wisdom of her teaching. Humiliated, I vowed to keep my musings a secret from the ignorance of my teachers.

Yet in sixth grade, playing the spelling game again provided me with a new opportunity. And after much deliberation, I dared to share my most cherished word: *essence*. When no one guessed it and the stick figure of the man was hung, my teacher, Mrs. Young, asked if I would be willing to fill in the letters and share with my classmates its meaning. With lyrical delight, my passion was told, held in a buoyant field of fullness. Its contagion touched a place so rich, so hidden that my classmates melted in the presence of their own essence, letting down all guard and allowing their preciousness to be seen. In a manner of minutes, my shy, introverted self went from having one friend to gaining many more who would quietly over the years confide in me their deepest secrets, meeting soul to soul, essence to essence. And so then, my friend, let us ask, What is *essence*?

Courting us is Intelligence, a gift of Being ready to unfold the instant we allow our awareness to join it. This knowing taps innate wisdom, which intrinsically reveals what is needed at any given point in time. Such unbiased, unconditional generosity of genius is the living guidance of our Being, a direct conduit of our infinite flow of Source. And all that is necessary is that we be present—but present to what?

Presencing the Essence of the Essence of Love

If we look at the definition of the word *presence*, it means "now." Masters for eons have been guiding us in the art of being here now.[4] Yet if presence is to be here now, then what is being? Looking at Webster's dictionary, we discover that *being* means "essence." So then to be *present* is actually "pre-essence." Presence is required to notice essence. Now, if *being* means "essence," what does *human being* mean? If we look at the words *hu-man-being*, we discover that *Hu* in Sanskrit means "love song to God." And in Webster's dictionary, *man* means "living soul," which means "essence." And *being* means "consciousness," which also means "essence." Furthermore, we discover that *essence* actually means "love"! Isn't it amazing that right here encoded in the very namesake given to us as a collective species there is a continual reminder of our true nature! Now if we are the *essence of the essence of love,* then what is this love the essence of? What is that which is subtler—so subtle yet unfathomably powerful, barely perceivable yet profound? What is minute yet infinitely expanded, free of self-imposed limitations in this coherent field of love?

These subtleties I speak of are the essential qualities that comprise the soul. This is the breath that breathes the breath,[5] the substance and quality of the subtle body of our soul. It both individuates us and unites us in the Oneness of ALL. Here at ground zero where the edges meet, who we once thought we were comes undone. And it is in this mechanism of slowing down and pausing in the still point of the fulcrum that—if we dare to open to the momentum flying us forward and simultaneously pulling us back——we can truly and directly experience the fuller essential expression of our True Self![6] It is here, at this edge, that——if we pause long enough to receive the gifting of these subtleties of essence the energies of our soul——we can perceive their medicine acting upon us, rendering us authentic by dismantling any false structure of identity.

And if we dare to accept this dance and allow it to move us, the gift given is beyond price. For what we are given is life. Not any kind of life. This is life as love co-creating itself, authoring itself...bright, flowering, and alive. It is an essential life, not the frenzied, feverish, or depressed way one feels when trying to catch up with or chase after life. But rather there resides within us a deep calm and depth of quietude, the infinite expanse of peace and assurance that arise from confiding in spirit. We are bestowed with a direct experience of spirit, and no force is more powerful than that of pure unconditional love.

From unadulterated loving truth, the subtle flirtation of one's essence whispers its love song. We respond, inviting awareness to open our eyes, to savor the scent, caress the intangible, and soar in her Grace. These gifts of being are infinitely bountiful. And once we bow to her glory and step onto her magic carpet, our life will never be the same.

And so, *breathe with love into the quiet center.* Remember who you are at this moment in time, on this earth, as a hu-man being; you are *the essence of the essence of Love.* It is here that you have an opportunity to directly know the true love that you *Be.* To fully embody the wholeness of your God-given capacity, then, is to experience the intrinsic nature of unity.

I am the incomprehensible silence and
the often-remembered thought,
I am the voice of many sounds and
the expression of many designs.
I am the utterance of my own name.
For I am Sophia of the Greeks
and the Gnosis of the barbarians.
The one who has been hated everywhere,
and loved everywhere.
I am godless and I am she whose godhead is multiple.
I am the one whom you have considered and
whom you have scorned.
I am unlearned, and it is from me that you learn.
I am the gnosis of my seeking,
and the finding of those who seek after me.

-- The Thunder, *Perfect Mind* (NHC VI, 2)[1]

Chapter 2

The Journey

Welcome. You are about to embark on a great adventure, and the adventure is you. Here you will pioneer a terrain vaguely remembered; yet with practice, each time you return, more of your true Self will be revealed.[2] As you continue to cultivate your connection with the essential healing qualities of your soul, you will learn more about how to navigate this subtle hidden terrain, developing powerful skills to further life-enhancing change.

Conditioning and False Beliefs

Our soul's essence uniquely highlights various aspects of the human journey. It sheds light on the confusion of the conditioning and false beliefs we have mistaken as our own. When we begin to recognize, discern, and differentiate our pure nature, that which is does not fall away, exposing the preciousness of our Being. Only then can true healing occur and the perceived separation of the ego and soul be experienced instead as whole. The subtle body of our soul is the substance of living Guidance, conscious Intelligence. It is the Innate Wisdom of our Authentic Self, the Beloved—–the Whole birthing potentiality, Love creating life ready to be actualized any moment. This is Source energy, the great Mystery, Grace. It is the divine poetry of our quantum nature. Ancient are these teachings; simple and direct is the Way.[3]

In the human potential movement, many systems and schools teach us to get in there, to reprogram and fix our beliefs, emotions, and pain. Yet no matter how much we do to get it right and solve the problem, it never seems to be enough. We may change to a certain degree, yet there remains hidden, buried, and unclaimed a treasure chest brimming with the bounty of our jeweled nature: *the Divine preciousness of Being*. Each jewel of essence, of embodied consciousness unlike any other, is ready to be claimed should we allow ourselves to melt all the way in and receive the gift of Self. Here nothing is lacking, nothing is lost.

What we discover is that without tapping into the wisdom of the Light and energy that we essentially are, we can become lost in a convoluting labyrinth of never-ending stories passed on to us through our early conditioning. These are the stories that we bought into, rejected, or were unaffected by in our attempt to get what we needed to survive. All of this, along with our DNA, is imprinted with history (his story and her story), the blueprint of our ancestors. This whole invites us to cultivate a deeper, fuller understanding of our Self. As suggested by Leonard Cohen's lyrics in "Anthem,"

> *Ring the bells that still can ring*
> *Forget your perfect offering*
> *There is a crack, a crack in everything*
> *That's how the light gets in.*

It is we ourselves who solidify our point of view, blocking out the light, passing on the impenetrable perfectionism of our limiting beliefs to our offspring and the ultimate creation of this world. Yet, like the fixative our adrenals secrete when activated by shock to stabilize an injury, so do outworn, conditioned patterns become the binding adhesion that restricts our very flexibility and freedom of movement. What was needed in the beginning no longer serves us.

We actually embed our power in our deficiency, and then we convince ourselves that our misbelief is who we are, defending the deficiency with all our might! Imagine that! No wonder we often feel crazy and don't understand what is going on. We are at a loss because our construct is so hidden, so convoluted, and so confusing. Which "I" am I, really?

To let in the light, the brilliance of Being exposes a crack, a chasm into an identity constructed upon the deficiencies of powerlessness, loss, lack, fear, shame, doubt, and guilt. To open and surrender to our effulgent radiance is to give up and let go of the old form we believed would protect us. Our true self can then come out of hiding! We are no longer driven by self-preservation based on a belief, which is actually a judgment based on a constructed identity about who we are and what is possible.

Defending Judgment

Our first clue, our first discernment that something is amiss is to see that the identity we are defending lives in judgment—all kinds.[4] *Being* needs no defending, is not lacking, does not judge. Being simply is unlimited possibility. So why is there such force and limitation around fragmented beliefs? The primary consensus among mystics and teachers in the field of consciousness is one based on a fundamental sense of separation——the original sin, falling from Grace. This stems from the humiliation of having a body with needs. Thus, the primary trauma is of being born into this world and feeling that I am separate from the power and presence of God. I am helpless.

From out of that sense of separation forms an altered ego. This ego structure is nothing more than an identity formulated upon the beliefs we've created around coping——strategies based on loss, hurt, inadequacy, fear, guilt, shame, and so on perceived through a feeling of lack. And the lack is nothing more than our identification with the ego deficiency because we have forgotten, hidden, or devalued our true nature, our essential self, our pure identity, which is the wholeness of our divine Beingness, the God spark within.[5]

Where it gets tricky is that the ego structure that formed around our helplessness and vulnerability became a would-be protector. But protecting what? Protecting our body and beliefs. In other words, this limited self-identity believes we are the body, and so it validates itself through tension, pain, and emotional entanglements.[6] And any attempt to get rid of the ego is met with extreme defensiveness. Viewed from our ignorance, this translates as trying to get rid of the ego. Simultaneously, death of the ego translates that our body will die. Telling oneself to get rid of the ego re-traumatizes the protective structure that formed out of trauma to begin with. And here's the kicker: If we don't kill it, then let's heal it! This infers that we are broken. So now we try to fix what's been made up based on the false perception of lack. But you see we aren't lacking. We are intrinsically whole in our natural state of being. All that happened is that our wholeness wasn't mirrored, valued, and remembered. So there is no fixing what is already whole.

What we need is a clear perception into those places we denied, hid, disempowered, and dissociated from, which ensured our survival in early life when these patterns were established. Only compassion, self-love, and appreciation will open the door to places where we ourselves created separation from Source. So here lies the invitation to reconnect what we have disconnected for whatever reason.

If the synapses in our brains aren't connecting, it doesn't mean that we don't have a brain. It is just that from point A to point B isn't connecting at this moment. And how would we even realize this section is unhooked? We know simply by seeing and sensing that nothing is there. There is a felt sense of vacancy, invisibility; we exist in a chasm, space, or void, which brings us back to the ego's deficiency. However, interpretation solely through the limitation of the deficiency brings with it a feeling of unsafety and terror be-cause the deficient identity doesn't know or remember the whole Self. From its point of view, any space is dangerous and interpreted as a loss, a lack, a hole. The more spaciousness there is, the less fixated the identity, which is perceived as annihilation of the perfected, controlled self.

In other words, there is a subconscious fear that if one unleashes the grip of control, space will open to annihilate the self as we know it. From this point of view, we will no longer exist. This is both true and not true. The rigidity that was familiar will release, but we will still be here, though a bit disoriented because the new version is less familiar. And so it will require practice and constancy to develop a new capac-ity of embodiment as we learn to trust the less-familiar dissolving and reorganizing integration process of our innate intelligence.

Discerning Between Spaciousness and Dissociation

We are now entering a territory where an understanding, experienced teacher would be beneficial. Although spaciousness and dissociation can look alike to a traumatized individual, a trained facilitator knows these are very different states. Dissociation is a shock response, a protective strategy to split off our awareness of the body to avoid feeling overwhelming sensations, emotions, and thoughts. It doesn't feel safe to be in a body. What current science has discovered is that fear is more in our body than in our mind.[7] Yet psychology will often address the fear as a product of the mind. The dilemma is that both the mind and body need to be presenced and validated to move through the perceived fear. However, it can be a charged edge because although the perception of spaciousness requires embodiment, it can also bring on arousal and panic.

This process needs time to evolve; it requires us to develop a new relationship with our self. Thus, it requires the practical cultivation of consciousness grounded in the body along with an expansive perceptual awareness of spaciousness at the same time. The latter is essential when integrating our personal identity, *the ego,* with Source Self, the *Being.* In other words, we are re-Sourcing ourselves. From this integral wholeness of Self-actualization, we are freed to live our lives authentically.

Still, an essential ingredient is often bypassed, which is the result of the alchemical transfiguration of elemental substances. These substances of our essential nature are the very stuff of King Solomon's treasures and Shambhala——often referred to as the *paradise of our dreams*, the jeweled nature of our essential Being. Nutritive substances of soul restore, regenerate, and inform new potentialities in mind-body-soul experience. Our lives become enriched in every way possible, and it is here that we can now experience true contentment and satisfaction in profound, yet simple ways. The ordinary becomes extraordinary, allowing us to live a blessed reality that is *real-i-tied*, that is *connected with our Source Self.* We are then able to have a conscious spirit-earth experience.[8]

Valuing and Receiving the Offering

And so it is vitally important that we appreciate, value, and receive these offerings of essence no matter how subtle or minute they may appear. For the old mind of the past will disregard, dismiss, and diminish anything that it perceives will threaten the fixation of its stance. Thus, an unwavering practice of constancy and clear perceptual integrity is necessary, requiring that we show up again and again, aligning with the simple truth of an awakened basic reality. We are in need of a unified matrix, a template from which it is possible to do our human tasks from the grounded groundlessness of Being. We are learning to integrate the original separation of the fundamental split in our identity, allowing us to be *holy here, wholy here*—a spiritual Being expressing Self through a human experience.

Within this body
Are enchanted fields and woods,
The seven seas and the innumerable stars.

Within this body
Are the touchstone and the jeweler.

Within this body
The Eternal keeps singing
And Its spring goes on and on flowing.

Kabir says, "Listen, my friend, listen——
My beloved Lord is within."

—— Kabir[1]

Chapter 3

Body, Soul, Creation History

L ike rootlets reaching into the depth and breadth of our somatic beginnings, our esoteric psycho-spiritual heritage can be traced throughout antiquity. Once cloistered in the coded secret teachings of the mystery schools to spare us from persecution, this sacred knowledge is being unveiled at momentous speed. We are now able to recognize that a universal secret is open should we be willing to participate in the conversation of mind, body, and soul. Our human race and the planet have reached a critical mass, and we are being trumpeted to awaken from the illusory trappings of victimhood, disempowerment, and fear. This paradigm shift, this spiritual renaissance is calling us en masse to join with the effulgent radiance of Grace, asking each one to step up to his or her part in sustaining sentient and non-sentient beings alike in an embodied co-creative partnership.

The lineage of our masters teaches us that to *know* the whole truth, we must include the knowledge of the body, wherein reside intelligences we have yet to fully fathom. Thus, many of the wisdom teachings expressly require any number of embodiment practices such as meditation, chanting, and exercises, as well as movement to develop self-mastery and freedom from the entrenched unconscious and habituated patterns of limitation that perpetuate our suffering.

The ancient teachings of the Vedic Upanishads beautifully express the necessity of accessing wisdom through the body, as implied by the two following quotes:

What you cannot know in your own body you can know nowhere else.

These words indicate that first we must show up and be present with being here. We must be with what arises in our physicality, the terrain. With practice, we can develop our awareness so finely that eventually we can touch into the level of our DNA. The scriptures then encourage us to further open our awareness to include spaciousness, for it is from out of space that matter, DNA, is born. The following maxim has long been known in the Vedic tradition:

The entire universe is in your body, and you need not be afraid of it.

We cannot trust our mental thoughts alone. Mental constructs are just that and create further separation. This form of alienation is akin to giving a toddler the steering wheel of a vehicle to drive without adult supervision. Mental musings are nothing more than beliefs we make up about ourselves or others, and they are based on images we ourselves create. These freeze-framed points of view originate from judgment, which creates isolation, which begets paranoia. As a result, there arises the need to control everything and everyone, for our delusion originally developed from a feeling of loss of control.

Here we get to meet our entanglements around fear and trust. One side cannot exist without activating the other, resulting in a fundamental conflict of relationship between our conditioned mind and the body's sensations. To help better understand this mechanism, let us turn to the following lesson by the fifteenth-century Indian Islamic scholar Imam-i-Rabbani, who clarifies for us the relationship of the soul's essence to the body. He explains the origin of our amnesia and the distortions around identity that have plagued mankind since time eternal by shedding light on the confusion about the Self and the mind-body relationship.

This Soul Essence was given the potential to evolve. But in order to improve it had to unite with the body. For this reason Soul was given an affection towards the body. It threw itself upon the body. And being fine and very expansive it sank and penetrated to all parts of the body. It forgot about itself. It came to think of itself as the body. As many people consider themselves only as bodies and so being unaware of the existence of the Soul, they disbelieve it.

—Imam-i-Rabbani[2]

Accessing Your True Nature

To access our essential nature——the finest, most subtle substance within us——we must drop into, meet, and be with the inner spaces and denser matter of the body. And to do this requires us to feel what is present in the moment. Whether coming as a belief or an emotion, some kind of sensation will occur at this point, even if it appears to feel like nothing. *Nothing* is actually a quality of space (for example, emptiness, invisibility, and so on) when viewed from the ego's perspective.

From this view, it will seem like nothing is there. Yet if we pause here long enough, our awareness will begin to awaken to more of what is really present. What seemed like nothing becomes more substantial, such as full space, denser space, fluid space, and so on. At this level, we meet the paradox. It appears as nothing while at the same time there is a potency that is barely perceptible. It doesn't go along with our regular way of thinking.

It is brilliant how cleverly the ego distracts us from perceiving what it fears will erase its existence. If you remember, the ego views itself as being the body. By allowing spaciousness into your awareness, you loosen the grip of tension that helps you feel like you have a physical form. The ego's identity is attached to feeling tension to reassure it that it exists; hence, the hamster wheel of going, going, going, doing, doing, doing——all to avoid being with what's not that!

Eventually though, we learn to trust the spaciousness, as well as cultivate the sensitivity to perceive it, thus healing this grave misunderstanding. Sensation brings with it every enchantment of the natural world and the cosmos——all of the elements and forces of creation that exist. And it is through the senses that we can access the subtle terrain of our essence, the organ of our soul. In doing so, we remember by nature's alchemical process, taking us from the egoistic defense of a false structure (appearing as the coarsest, thickest, heaviest matter) to the ecstatic celebration of our true essence (the most delicate, refined, barely perceptible substance).

As our capacity to be present grows, we become more and more conscious. When the Pharisees asked Jesus when the kingdom of God would come, he answered, saying,

The kingdom of God does not come with observation; nor will they say, "See here!" or "See there!" For indeed the kingdom of God is within you.

—— Luke 17:21, KJV

In other words, don't look outside of yourself. God is not external. We must look from within. In the design of the caduceus, which is often used as a symbol for medicine, one can vividly see a precise map of this principle laid out in plain view, a direct way to optimize our wellness as well as access the divine. Yet the medicine of the ancients does not resemble the medicine of today. Physicians commonly prescribe synthetic, non-biocompatible therapies, forgetting the esoteric truth behind the symbol. Many chemicals in current use are foreign to the body and can interfere with delicate physical mechanisms, such as the pineal gland's ability to balance the hormones of the endocrine system, which affect change of mood, metabolism, and sexual function, among other things.

The caduceus depicts two entwined snakes (*double helix of DNA*) around a central channel (*spine*) as they rise to become two wings (*lateral ventricles of the brain*), which are topped by a knob (*pineal gland*). We will explore this more elsewhere, but first let's take a look at *primary respiration*, a term coined by Dr. William Sutherland, D.O. (1873-1954), whose brilliant research and discoveries were influenced by Dr. Andrew Still, father of osteopathy (developed in 1874 and later adopted by the American Medical Association in what became the roots of osteopathic medicine), akin to cranialsacral therapy.

This method works with the fluid drive in our cerebral-spinal system. When balanced, it reflects organic tidal rhythms of oceanic nature.

Through the subtlest touch, a practitioner can monitor the glandular system, the brain, body, and its field. In balance, a healthy, uninhibited spine naturally rocks in a barely perceptible wave (referred to by Wilhelm Reich as the *orgon reflex)*, which was thought to derive from orgasmic-cosmic energy, meaning God-Source energy. This barely perceptible pumping system of spinal fluids creates a gentle wave up the spine and through the fluid-filled ventricles of the brain, where it stimulates the winged bone of the sphenoid that sits at the top of the spine, gently rocking it in a butterfly-wing motion like a figure eight turned on its side. And the reclining figure eight is the symbol of infinity.[3]

With this motion of the spine, the structures in the cranium as well as the glands of the brain are gently massaged through the reciprocal action of a subtle movement that encourages secretions such as serotonin, melatonin, and the like. The autonomic nervous system is thus regulated, which balances the arousal and rest mechanisms between the sympathetic and parasympathetic nervous systems. An hour-long cranial session can feel like hours of rejuvenating rest. The heart feels expansive and connected to All, and the crown chakra gently releases as it does when Shakti energy rises during kundalini yoga or other meditation practices. In recent times, offshoots of the original osteopathic cranial work address this beneficial fluid balancing, such as Ortho-Bionomy, Network Chiropractic and Emergence Care.

Coming Full Circle in DNA Research

Bear with me as I bring you along on a quick tour. If we go back in history to the creation of the human form that we now are, we find testament of our story in Sumerian cuneiform clay tablets (dating to 6,000 BC), which were unearthed all along the Tigress and Euphrates Rivers in the 1970s. These tablets speak of Anunnaki space travelers who came to earth to mine gold, which they alchemically altered into a monatomic white powder. It is written that when ingested, this nectar of *amrita* energetically transforms the fluids of the ventricles of the brain, symbolized by the caduceus' wings, awakening a person's inherent spiritual intelligence. This opening of the All-Seeing Eye or pineal gland further enhances the mind, body, soul connection. It's interesting to note that in the Tibetan language, the translation for the word *eye* is "far-reaching water lantern," an illuminated fluid light emanating in all directions simultaneously.

Researchers have discovered Sumerian gods, or space travelers, holding devices shaped like a pine cone, which is the same shape as our pineal gland. Was this used for time travel, teleportation, and intuitive telepathic communication as many have suggested? Tens of thousands of such Sumerian tablets have been discovered and are now being decoded by scientists and scholars. The story continues, according to these ancient tablets, that the Anunnaki extraterrestrial genes inseminated the ovum of an ape-like being and were then implanted in the womb of a birth goddess, an Anunnaki woman who became the mother.[5] Imagine the implications of such archaeological findings that radically disrupt the history we've been taught. The earth is not flat! And we have abilities far beyond our understanding!

Here I would like to mention the scientific research of Nobel Prize molecular physicist Francis Crick, who was the co-discoverer of DNA. He found that our DNA consists of an encoded, six-foot long, double helix crystalline strand coiled within every cell. According to Crick, all living organisms have shared the same DNA since the beginning of time. Scientists can also verify that our DNA is in fact the stuff of stardust. Meteorites that have fallen to earth contain DNA matching our own.[6]

Further, DNA is a substance much like liquid light. It has the ability to flow like a liquid yet exhibits the signature of a crystalline solid, an intermediate phase between liquid and solid. A team of physicists led by Chia-Fu Chou recently discovered this property of DNA, which emulates the precisely disordered manner in which essence transfigures an outgrown belief once realized, lighting up one's consciousness. We are truly growing in ourselves a new form––from solid, to fluid, to gas, to ether, and back to form again. The implications are astonishing when we consider the power of what appears to be spontaneous remission and other such healings. This brings us to the edge where consciousness creates matter, the domain whence essence comes. Our current era will finally honor the dance between form and formlessness. Beam me up, Scotty––for real!

In the first chapter, we saw that one meaning of the word *man* is "essence," and *essence* means "subtle energy." In Hebrew, the root meaning for *man* is "Adamah," as in Adam. *Adam* means "land" or "ground," making reference to the first man created out of atoms, a molecular structure. *Adamah* also means "blood." I will talk more about this in chapter 18. Furthermore, to add more to our mystery, when we look at the name inscribed in the cornerstone of Jerusalem's Holy Temple, we find the inscription YHVH, which when translated means "the timeless name of God." According to Gregg Braden's research, when the chemical equivalent of the three gases hydrogen, nitrogen, and oxygen is compared with the God code, there is only one letter that sets us apart. It is this letter that gives us our physicality, and that is carbon, which constitutes our DNA. So then, what we all have is *"God eternal within the body"*––the full meaning of the Hebrew letters decoded.[7]

Wearing the Charge of Our History

The Bible and the Qur'an speak of God as having created man out of dust. In somatic mind-body work, the common motto among practitioners is *the body remembers*. And in somatic and spiritual practices alike, the practitioner or teacher helps clients or students to get grounded in their body for positive change to occur. This sheds light on why it may feel uncomfortable to stay present with our body, because when we are somatically sensing, so much information comes forward that navigating all that can be overwhelming. Not only does the body wear the charge of our emotions but it is also imprinted with unconscious pathways encoded both in the DNA from our ancestors and our own embedded beliefs. It is interesting to think of what we are creating from the intersection of the two.

I remember my first Zen mediation practice when I was fourteen. It was excruciatingly painful to sit in one place with myself and to be present like that with my breath and my body. The sensation felt like knives cutting through my nervous system all over. There was nothing relaxing about it! The experience was incredibly overwhelming. I just sat in my pain and cried silently. And the more I tried to relax, the more intense the sensations and panic became. I will share more about what this is about as well as the relationship of pain and our body further on.

Returning to the topic of the third eye, the pineal gland is thought to be the juncture between the body and soul. Philosopher Rene Descartes (1596-1650) first introduced this concept when he asserted,

The image of sensory stimulus from the soul appears on the surface of the pineal gland.

The All-Seeing Pineal Gland

It is fascinating that the pineal gland is the same shape and made of the same viscosity and tissue as a normal eye. This organ actually has a retina with rods like in our eyes' retinas, which is oriented toward the heavens and referred to as the third eye. The pineal secretes a psychoactive chemical called DMT, which releases light by piezo luminescence. There are 100–300 such micro crystals per cubic millimeter in the gland, in themselves also a source of light. Although this gland has the ability to produce light, it also needs sunlight to function optimally. Moreover, it has the capacity of turning into a radio station without the use of external electricity.[8] From a communication standpoint, this makes the following more than a possibility:

As within, so without; as above, so below.

This quote is one of the seven principles of the ancient teachings of Hermes Trismegistus, purported author of sacred texts known as the Hermetic Corpus, the basis of Hermeticism.

Yet this refined communication system can be adversely affected. It has been well documented that when too much fluoride invades the body, it can encrust the pineal lens. Trace amounts of organic fluoride are necessary, but too much blocks the light as the pineal becomes encrusted. When the light is eclipsed, our hormone system is disrupted and cannot transmit essential information from one organ or tissue to another, resulting in imbalances such as fertility issues that can affect our ability to procreate.[9]

The meaning of *hormone* from the Greek root is "to put in motion, to awaken." Imagine that within us is our very own internal transistor radio and light transmitter, navigating us toward the light. We are kept "awake" by an inborn barometer orienting our personal light to the great Light. Isn't it interesting that the Arabic translation for *Bethlehem* is "Bayt Lahem (House of Flesh)"? And the story of Jesus tells us that the three wise men from the East followed the North Star to his birthplace, bringing gifts to the Son of God. If we look at the story's symbolism, we could surmise that the three wise men are symbolic of the three intelligence centers: the Head *Intellect,* the Heart *Emotion,* and the Belly *Instinct.* And when acting in consort, they orient us to our Point of Light, referred to in Sufism and other traditions as *the True Self, the North Star.*[10]

So when we both fully inhabit and observe as a witness the mind-body juncture, while bringing our awareness to the space in-between, our inner seeing opens, amplifying the light. As a result, we realize the embodied experience of our illuminated spiritual nature and the various nectars, qualities, and substances of our soul's gifts––our essence. Anyone familiar with Islamic prayer knows the three invocations, one to each of the three centers, turning us toward the One.[11] The early fathers of the Catholic Church also clearly understood their significance, for there stands in the Vatican courtyard a giant bronze statue of a pine cone. This artistic pineal gland sits atop the *axis mundi*, representing the spine. And written in the Bible so that we may not forget are these words, as spoken by Jesus:

The light of the body is the eye: if therefore thine eye be single; thy whole body shall be filled with light.

–– Matthew 6:22, KJV

And the luminous Epinoia was hidden in Adam....

—— John 20:25[1]

Chapter 4

The Imaginal World

I magination operates with intelligence much like the imaginal cells in biological terminology, by which the caterpillar dissolving within the chrysalis becomes a new form––the butterfly. Behind the scenes, the intelligent information for this process has always been available, even though its new appearance seems to have occurred magically. Just as in stem cells, the cells of the bone marrow can differentiate into any form needed, such as liver cells or heart cells. As Sufi scholar Henry Bayman so eloquently stated, "The purpose of becoming is to return to being." This is akin to the Sufi path of self-realization, which strives to make the unconscious conscious.

Likewise, we move from a mundane biological state to one in which we can access the soul's essence, which Sufi scholar Henry Corbin coined the *imaginal world*, the domain of the *five Divine Presences*. This is an intermediate world between God and the manifest in which the Presences appear on the surface as our five sense organs: vision–sight, listening–sound, savoring–taste, sensing–touch, and scent–smell. When we engage these senses in a subtle, total way, we are able to access the most hidden, secret teachings of our soul. From this understanding comes the name Terrain of Essence, an in-depth methodology that teaches folks how to navigate the landscape of the soul.

The particular form of practice I learned, and have been cultivating for nearly forty years, is an oral tradition passed along through the ages from teacher to student. As shared by my teachers Faisal and Hameed, and their teachers, we find its roots in Platonism, Buddhism, The Fourth Way, and Sufism. The wisdom kernels of this teaching also have merit in the Kabalistic and Gnostic teachings as well as principles of the Tao and Vedas. Many believe that this ancient, esoteric, psycho-spiritual embodiment practice originated from the Sarmoun Dargouh, which means "Court of the Bees, or the beehive." The Sarmouni Brotherhood members are often referred to as the collectors of honey because they have been cultivating, preserving, and passing along such wisdom since the time of the Great Flood. The honey is the substantive knowledge of our divine essence, the elixir of the soul. And as with any other substance, it can be passed from one flask (human being) to another, and in times when it necessary to further transmit, one can pass along the elixir of this knowledge, the direct knowing of our divine heritage.

Inquiring Into and Including What's Here

This practice is rooted in inquiry and is a beautiful way to bridge concepts we do not see clearly, don't understand, are charged about, or disconnect from in addressing the various concerns and conditions we wish to resolve in our lives. The way of direct knowing is a practice I have deeply experienced and lies at the root of my own teachings. It can be applied to our everyday ways and life in these modern times.

The following is a simple example of how the Terrain of Essence practice is useful, for example, when experiencing pain. In this scenario, let's say there is a pain in my neck. Perhaps I keep treating it as a physical symptom. I seek all kinds of professional help, such as doctors, painkillers, massage, chiropractic, exercise, or some other, yet the pain persists. So now I reach out to someone who practices subtle inquiry work. With this method, many entry points are possible, but let's say that the first thing I'm asked is to notice and locate the pain. When I locate it, I detect a sharp sensation. That is one of the senses——sensation, which is a felt sense? To include all of the five senses means that I will also need to discover the shape, the size, the color, and the texture of what is present——all perceived through my sensory organs.[2] Remember, the soul is mingled with the terrain of the body. By exploring in this manner, I am led to what has not been apparent, which is revealed through the light of perception. I know it is sharp, but what about the texture and the rest of the environment, such as the scent, taste, or tone?

To access this subtle field, I will need to rest down into my body, expand my awareness, and meet what is here in my internal environment, letting go of trying too hard. It will be beneficial to simply allow my mind to float, because the information needed for resolution resides in-between the body and the mind. The more I try to concentrate or figure it out, the more I create blockage, which creates separation from true meaning. It can't be figured out with the head alone. What is required is that I be here with what is present rather than effort to do something about it. I will have to drop any preconceived idea and be present, including noticing body sensations. In this way, what is deeper can rise to my awareness. In cranial work, we call this dropping below mental concepts; we simply meet what is here and remain present with it while observing everything. This allows the innate healing mechanism already alive and eager within us to respond and self-correct. The result will be much more effective if we don't get in the way!

Next, I not only feel a sharp pain but also sense a red-hot poker. As I stay present to this, I sense that the pain is seemingly made out of metal. All of my senses are engaged in directly perceiving other nuances of the environment. I began with a sensation, and then got a visual impression, along with other sensory perceptions. Next, I noticed tension arising and activation of agitation. I brought my awareness to my breath, breathing, presencing, and resting in.

Pauses and gentle pacing are important. Now I notice anger. I'm feeling a charge to this emotion, and the charge is building, and it is getting more uncomfortable to be here. The more I stay here, the more anger I feel. I begin to feel overwhelmed by the charge of flooding sensation and find that I need to back out of this; it is getting to be too much. When I'm ready, I can check in again with the sensations. Less is more, and slow is helpful.

So now I have more information. There is actually an emotional underpinning to my physical pain. By being with that, and not making up a story about it or pushing it away, insight has been revealed. Treating it as merely physical cannot remedy the emotional component. And if what is underlying this charge is not allowed, the interference remains, and so continues the pain. In this case, the emotions need to be welcomed, too.

Sensing and Perceptual Tracking

This example just touches the surface of the process to illustrate the value of including our senses. It began with being present to the physical sensation. The last chapters in this book have two more samples of tracking and inquiry. One begins with a limiting belief and the other explores the emotions. Each of these inquiries concludes with an integrated sense of wholeness.

When all five senses are included in tandem, we have full access to our intuition, our greatest perception. Intuition induced in this manner sheds light so that what is innermost can be seen. At the same time, the divine light of Source is guiding the process. We experience a connection between above and below through the fractal nature of the all-seeing eye of intuition, which expands our wisdom. Through the felt sense of being in a body, the personal essence of our soul is revealed. And the essential quality of true substance will be exactly what is necessary to resolve what our defensive reaction has been unsuccessfully imitating.[3]

In other words, the more limited the belief, the more likely there will be a reaction. For example, anger is difficult to be with. And if the person has not developed a larger capacity to witness, allowing him or her to see the bigger picture as well as sense the charge of anger and what it is really about, and then he or she may be inclined to act it out by creating an argument, a fight, or an internalization of the frustration to avoid the deeper feelings. Or one may create separation from it altogether by splitting it off. If I don't feel the charge, then I can't be angry––a landmine in the making!

Yet if we look at anger, what does anger want? Ultimately, it wants to connect. And when we feel a driving need to connect, this usually shows up as passion. However, the bigger truth is that even if we do connect, driven by a need outside of our self, it will not suffice because our drive is but an imitation of what is truly needed. Our salvation is in connecting with our Source self, the *Beloved*––the light of all that we *Be* and a higher octave of our passion. If we develop this skill, we can actualize the very essence we are longing for.

But it won't work to skip over one level to get to the other. We have to presence whatever is here along the way, meeting all the nuances. To partner with Self will greatly simplify one's life! Then, whoever it is in this world that we decide to connect with is off the hook from having to provide All we want. When we fall in love and feel that delicacy and lightness of being, we can be assured that it is us——the grace of our essential self. Fall in love...with yourself, and don't stop!

Noticing What's Below That

Again, take the pain in the neck, for example: First is the noticing of the pain, next is the feeling of anger, and then is noticing that the anger is actually masking hurt feelings. Now, when the hurt feelings are allowed in a pure way, the heat that intensified can dissipate, and the act of showing up for oneself provides a natural state of love. When self-love is embraced, a full-embodied sense of strength arises. With this inner strength comes the excitement of being fully alive——an enlivened, rich, juicy sense of oneself.

An alchemical process has occurred, beginning with the reaction. Our example shows it beginning with an emotion and then dropping into the heart of the matter, claiming the truth of that. Then we notice the mechanism of projecting out what feels uncomfortable, along with not knowing how to be with it or what to do with all that charge, which is being with the mystery. This brings us directly in touch with the interface of seeing that it is we ourselves who are actually doing what we are insisting the other is doing to us.

For instance, one of the many insights could be that, at the heart of the matter, we are abandoning speaking our truth and feeling hurt around that, and then we blame others. Thus, we then are distracted away from feeling the hurt. And so, what really needs to be felt here is our own shame around self-betrayal. When that is felt, and the heat of it permeates the body, the essential cure occurs.

As the heat eases, we may begin to feel a rich lusciousness, a juiciness, an aliveness. Most likely, as a child we didn't feel safe being this alive or expressing it, so we have learned to cut off the experience, to deny it. The essence of Self is the vitality of this juicy aliveness,[4] free to be actualized in whatever expression is needed to maintain the integrity of wholeness. To realize this *is* the healing.

I want to reiterate that this sequence of happening doesn't mean going wild and acting out in a way that is not integral. If your response is driven by any of the three centers separately, then it's not coming from wholeness. Wholeness is not driven by a grasping need, nor is it stuck in a stance. The substance of the healing itself is the provision from the soul to integrate the mind-body-soul connection. You could say that not only does one have access to inner wisdom but also to the inner healer, *our inherent physician of the soul.* These are one and the same, allowing the transmutation to take place.

Having a Safe Place to Dissolve and Assimilate

Spiritual practice, or opening our awareness and assimilating the mind, body, soul relationship so that we can experience more congruence, is like the journey of the caterpillar. Like the caterpillar, we initially go from one plant to the next, from one technique to another, gathering sustenance from outside sources. We are not yet aware of what we have to offer if we awaken to and embody the gold that is within. In this work, the gold is our value, our sense of self-worth. As with the caterpillar, at a certain stage of growth we need to choose a safe place to land. Here we can rest into a supportive environment to hold that which is unfolding.

There comes a time on the spiritual path when the student, like the pupa, needs to be held in a safe container where the old form can dissolve, grow, and differentiate. Melting, morphing, and transmuting is the step wherein the head joins the heart, the heart becomes tenderized, and the hardened structure of outgrown beliefs liquefies and becomes transformed. A different form occurs through an alchemical process in which one is no longer bound to earth but is given wings to fly, to freely navigate both heaven and earth. The spirit, free, is thus embodied, providing fuller and deeper expressions of being. Upon becoming a butterfly, we've outgrown the need to consume life. We instead begin to grow life by gathering and spreading pollen, while simultaneously sipping nourishing nectars and engaging in the co-creation of life. Now we can enable the fruiting and blooming of life and, at the same time, be fed by life. We finally grow up, joining the abundant cycle of existence, where giving is receiving and receiving is giving. There is plenty for all and contentment in knowing Self.

It is through our subtle organs of perception that we can access the limitless, timeless knowledge of our divine nature.[5] It is here I shall focus my work. The Vedic energy system of the chakras, from the base to the third eye, reveals the nature of duality. When our inner sight opens, the crown chakra opens, revealing our nondual nature, the nature of One. So from the pineal gland upward, we experience our unified nature. Where people get stuck and suffer is by skipping the lower chakras and, either through drugs or dissociation, going out the crown to this beautiful feeling of oneness. But when they come back to earth, all hell breaks loose. To really do the work, we have to access all of it and willingly open to and expose the places where we split off our awareness and go unconscious.

The pain of duality is mirrored back to us through all kinds of negative, uncomfortable situations. Yet when we do choose to show up and are willing to be responsible for our part, we will over time become more and more integrated. The integration is what the Sufis refer to as being in the world but not of it. This is symbolized by the five-pointed star, which represents man as a whole being––head in the heavens with outreached arms signifying the horizon, above and below in view with both feet on the earth, and living a physical reality as a multidimensional being.

Section Two

Repeating Patterns

In honor of death, I took to the mountains——
Again and again I meditated on the uncertainty
of the hour of death,
Capturing the fortress of the deathless unending nature of
mind.
Now all fear of death is over and done.

—— Milarepa[1]

Chapter 5

My Story

The year is 1972. I am alone in my apartment when I hear a knock at the door....

Cold, dead wood pressed against my cheek, heart racing, veins pumping, crazed with horror. Airway immobilized, louder and louder the deafening cacophony of vital organs laboring against 200 pounds of crushing hate pinning my neck to the floor, knife blade poised to carve. Accomplice joins the taunting, drug-laced madness, tying ankles and wrists behind and around my neck, cinching tighter and tighter still yet. Left for dead, I feel my brain coming out of my head. In and out of consciousness I go, rasping, rattling; fading as vital organs are shutting down, like giant tankers beached in the ground, engines revved with nowhere to go. Far, far, far away a faint echo of sobbing murmurs deep down within the crippling thought of drowning in my own blood. Pressure welling, slamming against grief-filled anguish...I am too young to die.

My life is flashing before my eyes at sonic speed; cross-tides intercede, and I am swept, swept away in a sea of unfathomable love. Undulating waves are swelling, rolling in, filling up the depth of my love for all those close to me. Those still alive and ones who have passed appear, welcoming and assuring me. I can see everywhere; nothing is hidden. In turn, I am buoyed and filled by their love returning toward me, embracing me. My heart is dilating; full the river spills with goodbyes, remorse, and tears––the weighted sadness of leaving behind those I love so dear and near. Their images fade, and gaining speed I am moving through a narrow tunnel, then thrust out into a vast sea of darkness engulfed in infinite black––pending.

Here everything stops: sounds of my body, torment of my thoughts, struggle and torturous pain. Everything is gone, gone away, and I am suspended in silent eternity. Here there is nothing, no sense of a self. Timeless, weightless, nothingness. . .as though "I" have been erased… Yet, awareness remains.

Looming… a force of radiant intelligence, of luminous power condensed and compact gathers me in, I am propelled with lightning speed. Ascending, they rise rapidly toward me, flanking me, escorting me––two majestic angelic beings. . . light upon light, a dazzling dimension of brilliance. Awed by their presence, their beauty, their essence, I realize we are pure luminescence. We are the light. We are communicating not by words, but we understand. I feel an immense empirical peace, an infinite release of exhilarating joy and freedom, heart quickening with expectant excitement the nearer we are. The force pushes back, yet we are absorbed.

We are entering the sun, intensely brilliant, fusion unveiled, incomprehensibly powered magnificence. Benevolent love washes through me from everywhere at once. Divine Grace is all there is; I am it, it is me. Extreme exquisite beauty, arching and overarching rainbow fractals, a matrix of loving light beyond anything I've consciously known. Once again, narrowing, centering, readying. . . and I ascend through the eye of the needle, through the dome of this grand mandala, projected onto yet another sphere. . .sound and light intensified, amplifying celestial choirs here and afar.

I am aware of a coalescence and a boundlessness of Being——a mightily roiling, generative Presence; an enormous thundering; a blinding, arcing of neon eminence beyond this golden radiance. Churning at the edge, treading at the threshold of an ineffable grandness, heart quickening, welling with anticipation, I ask, "May I cross?

Bellowing Compassion booms back, "Not now. It is not time for you."

I am stricken with grief. "Please, may I come in?"

Once again my Lord commands, "Go back now; return. You have work to be done."

As though severed...I come crashing down with lightening speed back into the weighted earth...of my body. A swollen denseness, suffocatingly apparent under the immovable heaviness of grief and disappointment beyond what I can bear, fills me as I awaken in groggy confusion of thickened air. My name is being called with urgent distress, hands pushing hard against my chest. Smelling salts. They are shaking me, slapping my face, commanding me, "Come back now!" And I return...overwhelmed, in shock. I've returned to hell.

I was age eighteen, newly living on my own in San Francisco when this assault and robbery occurred in my apartment flat——two weeks before my audition for the modern dance company in which I would dance for many years. And two weeks earlier, having been drugged, kidnapped, and ending up in a terrifying situation, not knowing how I got there, I had become an expert in living with pain and confusion.

I remember wondering as a child how, if it felt so terrible then to have a body, how would it be by the time I grew up. How would I possibly be able to endure even more suffering? From early childhood, I had alternated between sharp and dull pain in my neck and back, but greatest was the impenetrable numbness cast around my heart and wrapping my brain. I dragged the weight of my inner corpse with loyal unyielding perfectionism, overriding the exhaustion I chronically wore. What the world saw was a fine athlete and lovely dancer, racing through life challenging physical limitations, willing her body by pushing beyond its means. Thus, I relentlessly overrode the pain without rest.

Collapsing Control

After twenty-four years of reenacting the momentum of my birth trauma, my body finally reached a tipping point, collapsing under the duress and grueling precision I had demanded of it. It was my sixth year with the modern dance company, and the performing season was over for a few months. Summer dance camp had begun, bringing in students from all around the country. I was front and center, demonstrating a *grand battement*, kicking my leg high into the air. At the peek of the movement, it was as though a guillotine had severed my limb at the hip. After a flash of excruciating pain, the dead weight of my leg thudded to the floor. There I stood upright in shock and disbelief, helpless as uncontrollable convulsions rolled up and down my body. My core turned icy, my face on fire. There was nothing I could do.

I, who had prided myself with having impeccable control of my muscles, now could not move. I was hostage in my own body as it shook of its own accord. My body had cracked, and my psyche broke at the damnation of its sentence. Walls kept spinning while the rest of the room stood still, everyone frozen in place. After an eternal moment, I began leaning into the assistance that was offered, inching across the dance floor one foot after the other in what felt like forever. That day my dancing career ended, after twenty of my twenty-four years. Dance was what I knew myself by, and now it felt as if my whole world had ended. Gone was the person I took myself to be. Gone was my identity.

And so began my real work, launching my journey toward self-realization. Powered by the accumulation of past traumas and injuries, I was compelled to receive, explore, and train in dozens of healing modalities, learning to recognize and integrate the separation I had created among the functions of my mind, body, and emotions. Alas, I was face to face with the ultimate separation I myself unknowingly had imposed between my egoistic and spiritual identities. Although my professional dance career had ended, what felt like a tragedy in reality would gift my jump into lifelong discovery and, eventually, the profound resolution of pain and suffering.

Little could I know at the time that my love of movement was not ending, but evolving into a more subtle form. And through this awakening came the appreciation and understanding of the physics of movement I had long experienced through dance. My love of the structure of movement would become the fresh template I needed to incorporate the development of a new, pure, and simple form of perceiving the unconscious underpinnings of the human coping mechanism, which often devises false meanings to survive. This was accomplished through the detailed tracking of energetic movement, wherever it could be found.

Reaching Out for Help

The next twenty-year chapter of life involved studies ranging from those of spiritual masters, shamans, faith healers, psychic surgeons, medical intuitives, and psychological, somatic, and psycho-spiritual adherents to a multitude of protocols featuring body and energy work and trauma resolution. While in the Touch Trauma Resolution of Injury work with Kathy Kain, I recognized I had been living with posttraumatic stress and brain injury my entire life. The first clue came when I realized that I had been in fourteen car accidents within twenty-two years——crazy but true!

I had endured two sets of three accidents each, and once, two incidents in the same year. I was surprised when I put those facts together in sequence but did not consider the events as having any special significance. After all, I neither had stitches nor anything broken, so I must not have been too injured. What harm could a little fender bender do? Yet, I learned later, the effect of an impact while in a 2,000-pound vehicle going 25 miles an hour is equivalent to that of riding a bicycle off the roof of a second story building. And the shock of such a collision is equivalent to 300 pounds of pressure per square inch.[2] I had been taught, like so many of us, that if you fall off a horse, just get back on. I came from the school of hard knocks, which preaches that no pain means no gain. As I became more aware, however, I began to trace back to the times when my energy had been punctuated in a harmful way.

Discovering the Esoteric Essence Work

It was through the esoteric psycho-spiritual essence work with my primary teachers, Faisal Muqaddam and Hameed Ali (A.H. Almaas), that I learned to connect with my awareness in an embodied way, thus developing discernment of mind, body, and spirit. Along with the subtle touch modalities of cranial sacral work, Ortho-Bionomy, and Touch Trauma Resolution, I could actually begin to be present with the intense terror and fear stored in my system without running away. Little by little, the hidden content in deep freeze began to thaw and rise, helping me to see what was there and over time connect the dots. Through this painstakingly slow process, my brain began to heal, and the pain lessened a bit each day. With the pressure releasing and dropping in, I learned to rest more into my body, to be present, to stay and not to freeze or fly away.

The process of going back through life events that held a particular charge, and then taking these back to their earliest origin, centered around two significant events: my premature birth and my kidnapping at age two. Noting this, I began to see how the series of later traumas was but a reenactment of earlier situations. They were showing up now as particular patterns throughout my life.

Slowing Down and Pausing

I am sharing this about myself simply to illustrate how we can go about our lives unaware that we have any part in what happens to us, until we realize that if we were awake and had the tools, the outcome could be different. When we slow down and take another look, what has been too much for the brain to process amid the overwhelm of traumatic events can then be accessed, seen, understood, and integrated. Yet, if we unconsciously continue our defensive or offensive behavior, we don't safely land, and so the nervous system doesn't get a chance to discharge, rest, or regulate.[3] As long as we are in a reaction formation, which is a way of coping with the overwhelm, we are not healing the disconnection.

> *Coping is a way to manage deficiency and*
> *stress, but it can't heal them.*

And so the stress continues to build, as in my case, until it reaches a tipping point, which can manifest in a variety of ways, such as addiction, disease, breakdown, depression, suicide, and aggression. It took years for me to even begin to comprehend the magnitude of impact my near-death experiences had had on me, let alone everything else.

Repeating-the-Story Trap

A tricky edge here is that once we've remembered what has happened to us, through the retelling of our story over and over, we are actually perpetuating the intensity of fear and reactivity. In other words, we are the ones who are now re-traumatizing ourselves.

> *Being a victim is not what happened to us.*
> *Being a victim is what we do to hold on to the pain.*
> *What happened has happened, whatever it was.*
> *Victimization is attaching our identity to the incident*
> *And defining ourselves according to that.*

A curious fact is that the brain responds to this repetitive behavior as it would with any other addictive stimulant. The word *addiction* is derived from Latin and means "enslaved" or "bound." Addiction hijacks the emotional pleasure area of the brain, the amygdala. And then the hippocampus, which is the part of the brain that stores and organizes memory, lays down the pattern. Thus, compulsive repetition lays down a memory pathway, creating an automatic conditioned response, and then floods the brain with dopamine. Dopamine is a neurotransmitter that regulates movement, emotion, and motivation. This chemical interacts with another neurotransmitter, glutamate, to take over the pleasure-reward circuit. So now we have added full-blown addiction to our fear. Because the brain can't tell the difference between fear and pleasure, it stills gets the reward——and wants more!

What can you do about that? Well, for starters, catch yourself in the act of the momentum of retelling your story, and drop it like a hot potato! You have got to interrupt the momentum. Not fun. It's like throwing cold water on an orgasm! Try it, and discover what it would be to rest back and breathe the Four-Square-Breath. This has been taught by Vedic mystic masters for millennia——four by four by four by four. More recently, the trauma community has embraced it.

Re-sourcing Trauma Breath

—— Inhale 4 counts

—— Pause 4 counts

—— Exhale 4 counts

—— Pause 4 counts

It can be 4 counts or 6 counts, more or less, depending upon
your own pacing, but you need to regulate it mindfully.
May this serve you well. Just remember to
STOP and DROP and BREATHE.

This breathing exercise is effective and simple. We will still feel the charge, but we aren't giving it the same meaning. It is important to breathe slowly, more softly, stepping out of the process if it feels like too much sensation or gets too scary. This is not a time to challenge or push through, or else we might end up recreating the mistrust and reinforce the same old pattern. Empowerment comes with tiny steps that accumulate and grow over time, building the capacity to stay present longer and longer as time goes on.

Now let's include more resources you can add to your re-sourcing practice to support self-care.

Sit or lie down and rest your back against a solid surface:

This supports the large muscles and encourages them to rest down. When we are endangered, these are the muscles we use to kick or run: the illiopsoas, gluteals, and quadriceps. The illiopsoas muscles attach along the spine from the diaphragm to the pelvis and are the largest, thickest muscles of the body. The gluteal muscles are those of the buttocks, and the quadriceps are the large muscles of the thighs. Notice as you move more and more into a natural, rhythmic breath how these muscles let go and rest.

Touch resource:

You may find that placing your hands on your body for comfort and contact to be supportive. What is comforting will be different for everyone. Perhaps you will like your hands on your belly, diaphragm, heart, or face. The warmth of the hands can emit the most far-infrared rays

(FIR) of anywhere on our body. FIR is a beneficial healing radiant heat wavelength of invisible light photons.

Cozy under a blanket:

Wrap in or under a cozy blanket and rest. In general, the more weighted the blanket the more calming the effect. You can also use a pillow and place it over the belly or on your lap. The sensory input of this warming contact releases serotonin in the brain. This chemical is a neurotransmitter that creates a feeling of calm and well-being.

Hot water bottle:

For added comfort, relief, and release, use a hot water bottle. Place it behind your neck to warm the brainstem or on your kidney area, which is at the base of the ribs on the back. Or, put the heat on the soles of your feet, or on your diaphragm and abdomen. These are all areas that will help to regulate and balance the nervous system, bringing a feeling of peace and rest and soothing the adrenals.

Create an ambient environment:

Calming music, candlelight, lovely scents, and beauty also help to create a healing environment and peaceful sanctuary. You can also reach out to health practitioners for tinctures, homeopathic support, or essential oils to assist your healing transition.

We are teaching ourselves a new way of being by providing the nurturance and loving support that was missing or not consistent in our lives. As a result, we learned to not attend and care for ourselves. This new way is still a mystery, for we've not gotten to fully know it yet. You may feel the body shiver or quiver as it discharges what has been stored in the body and not been released. This is a natural response, so be sure to be aware of your breath and to gently breathe. Tell no stories or stories about your stories, please. By this I mean to just be aware. You can watch the story unfold about what's releasing, but don't solicit it or grasp onto it or escalate it. Turn the persistence of insistence toward all-seeing awareness rather than getting swallowed in limiting identification. Be a witness.[4] Be present. Be the adult and loving presence that you have needed.

The more we catch ourselves in the act and practice this new way, the more our fear can release and melt into quiet, calming peace and the nature of love, for this is who we naturally are. By interrupting the old pattern, we are building trust between the mind and the body to support a new pathway. Fear is a primitive survival response,[5] needed only in moments of danger. Yet the mind keeps attaching story to what has happened long after the incident is over, which erringly perpetuates fear-based responses and keeps outworn sensory patterns running through the body.

This doesn't mean that that you can never tell the story of what happened. Rather, it's about gaining more capacity to be present and conscious by not getting swept away in identifying with and indulging the story. It's the escalation of the story, the run-away response that gets us in trouble. Eventually, your story may actually be a healing outlet for others. But until you are aware of the impulse driving your process, it's best to slow down and re-source yourself.

Then she gave one last burst of music. The white moon heard it, and she forgot the dawn, and lingered on the sky. The red rose heard it, and it trembled all over with ecstasy, and opened its petals to the cold morning air. Echo bore it to her purple cavern in the hills, and woke the sleeping shepherds from their dreams. It floated through the reeds of the river, and they carried its message to the sea.

—— Oscar Wilde, *The Nightingale and the Rose*[1]

Chapter 6

Loss, Identity, Momentum

Personal experience from an early age had taught me not to speak up for myself because I had nearly lost my life this way on several occasions. I had carried forward deeply embedded fear from those terrifying encounters, which shaped self-abandonment default mechanisms.[2] And due to an unfortunate series of circumstances, by the time I was age two, I had already lived with five different families. The only constants were the sweet smell of hay and moonlit nights against the backdrop of coyotes yelping beyond the crickets' choir.

Then one day she arrived, but I don't know her anymore. She puts me in a car and drives away, a long way away. I want to go back to the farm, ranches, golden hills, and Indian land. I want the almond trees, horses, cattle, and sheep. But she keeps driving. And gone is everyone I ever knew. Gone is the open sky of blue. Gone is the fiddling, the pony, the little boys, and the memories——erased and buried, and not to be spoken of ever again.

I arrive in a new home with a mother I don't remember and a man I don't know, and I am told he is my dad. But I know my dad, the one who visited me and took me out to ride on his horse when I lived with the different families. But she insists that is not true, and I have to bury and hide my truth deep inside, like a corkscrew wound below my mind. Eventually, I forget who I am.

That momentous departure was a half-day away from our arrival in the concrete gray coldness of San Francisco. Here I feel alone, isolated, and abandoned yet one more time in my ongoing experience of loss.

There is a new lady now. She comes when mom is away. She calls herself Mammy. Her skin glows like the moonlit night, black and shiny; her arms are full and soft, and she holds me in a way I've never known. She sings to me, pressed against her bosom; her voice is smooth and rich. I feel safe with her. She is love. Now she too is gone, and I miss her so much.

Teetering on the edge of the railing, the three-year-old me stands alone in my Zorro cape. I've climbed upon the overturned wash pail, mounted the porch railing, and decided to fly across the yard to the other flat where the Italian family lives. I hear them laughing and smell the yummy foods that scent the air. I want to live there. My people are gone and busy, and no one is here for me here. With one foot atop of the rail, I am up-stretched, my wings spread. I step off my second-story perch, flying to my new home.

My consciousness is slowly returning. Mom says we are home now and that I was in the hospital. She tells me that I have fallen and been unconscious. I hurt all over. My bones—— all of my bones hurt like a bad toothache in dull cold pain. My wings failed. I don't want to tell anyone I could not fly. I don't want to have a body anymore. I feel so ashamed of having not flown.

As a result of this adventure, I spent the next twenty years of my life perfecting my flight by being the grandest jumper in the dance company. I soared above the men, leaping with lofty *ballone*, with *tour jetes* and *grand jetes*, suspending myself in the air long gone before I would land. Each time I was floating closer to God; dance had become my prayer.

Trusting Ourselves

When I first began working with Faisal as his client in 1979, he often said that he had not met anyone who carried so much fear. I was surprised by his remark because I had not imagined myself to be afraid. Yet through the sessions, as I learned how to rest my mind and be present with my body, what had been buried began to surface. I got to feel the bracing effects of fear as painful memories emerged. In the somatic work, we say that *the body remembers; it never forgets*. It's true. Our mind can deny, avoid, and make up stories about our experience, *but the body doesn't lie*.[3] And so,

> *The truth about trust is in trusting oneself.*

We learn to trust, to be present with the information the body remembers and not to falsify it. But when we are cut off from the true experience of the body and still function from automatic pilot, no one is home. We are just using the body like a machine, driven by ego's mental commands. Our emotions go on acting out their unrefined charge. This raw movement is the energetic pattern that has been laid down in the body.

Considering the Law of Attraction

Now think of the law of attraction. In physics it is said that like attracts like. So whatever the energy, whether we are conscious of it or not, we get to have more of that until we become conscious of our unconscious choices. If we are unconscious of what we do, say, or believe, then we may make up all kinds of stories trying to explain why these things are happening. This is how we recreate the grooves we get stuck in. We paint ourselves into a corner and stick our heads in the sand——or use other persuasive tactics to avoid the full truth.

To consider what is true would expose our vulnerability, which could feel shameful, humiliating, scary, or confusing. Therefore, we are stuck in old patterns until we can fully be with and presence any trace of charge or sensation in the body without prejudice, avoidance, judgment, or corrupting the truth. Nevertheless, from here we can grow the seeds of self-love and compassion. This is the launch pad where real healing begins.

In those early years, I used my body to dance, but I wasn't embodied. Ironically, it was because of this numbing split that I could continue dancing through grueling performances with a fractured foot, bursitis in both Achilles tendons, shin splints, tendonitis, and more. Under the burden of such exhaustive self-punishment, along with carrying deep unconscious guilt for my existence, I unknowingly treated myself as dispensable and undeserving. I wasn't even aware of what I was doing, for I was identified only with rising above it all——flying high, up and out of my body to reach a God somewhere out there.

All my existence had been laid down unconsciously through an early pattern: every family I had lived with during my first two years of childhood had endured some kind of health crisis. To my little mind, something bad would happen when I came to live with others. I err-ingly associated their suffering with it being all about me. Hidden in the unspoken recess of my child-mind was the feeling that I was a jinx, that my very presence would cause others harm. It took me years to put words and meaning to those illusive feelings.

Trauma began in my mother's belly. She was performing in rodeos—trick riding, barrel racing, and breaking bucking horses—all while un-knowingly pregnant with me. She got gored in the forehead with the horn of a Brahma bull and was hospitalized, where she learned that I was five months along. I was born at seven months, premature and blue, strangled by the umbilical cord around my neck as a result of yet another accident...

Lightning cracks, cattle break loose. Mom and Dad take flight by horseback, rounding up the crazed stampede. Gone is all sense of direction in the freezing January blizzard. Thunder overhead, her horse spooks and tumbles, crashing down, down into the icy creek. Mom is unconscious...,'Lil Nell pinning her under. Struggling, Dad frees her limp body, throws it overtop his saddle in the frigid air, then rides us off Mount Shasta to the little town of McCloud, miles and miles away...

The momentum of my unwanted conception and traumatic birth con-tinued to haunt me, as did my parents' divorce when I was eight months old and, shortly after, my mom's failed suicide attempt. She had moved out of our mountain trailer and into town to fulfill her college scholar-ship. We stayed in a sorority house full of young women studying and partying. Somewhere in all the commotion my care fell through the cracks. Girls covering for each other thought I had been attended to, unaware that my insistent crying had been met only with being shaken, buried in pillows, and ignored while burning bedsores from sitting in the wet accumulated.

My mom, an honor student, was determined to do it all, and it was all too much. So my dad got custody and took me away, resulting in a struggle between my parents. Back with mom in her overwhelm, I was present when she decided to end her life. My young mind formed the belief that it was she who didn't want me. And so, between my birth parents and the family I joined at the age of two, I would eventually live in five different homes with five different groups of people. As I was passed from one family to another, each went through some kind of crisis, sending the message to my young mind that I wasn't wanted or worthy of being loved. I felt like an orphan, a throw-away that nobody wanted.

Eventually back with my mother, I grew up re-traumatizing myself through dozens of accidents.[4] I catapulted my body through space with sheer abandon in dance, water-skiing, and gymnastics, always taking risks, pressing the edge. This syndrome continued in my marriage to a race-engine builder, who had designed a barely legal street machine that could out run the cops. All the while, I was performing with the modern dance company and had entered an acting and modeling career, through which I continued to live my life with one foot on the gas and the other on the brake in a freeze-run-freeze pattern. After a prolonged, intense ride of alternating exhilaration and exhaustion, I ultimately was faced with fibromyalgia and chronic fatigue.

Changing Means Seeing What's Here

To change, we must first see what is here. To dream of wanting things to be different but not to know what we are doing has no legs. We need to be grounded in clear reality, otherwise our future is happenchance and not sustainable. Real support requires that we show up and take a sober look at the reality of what's really here under all the glam and glitter.

Recently, a student asked about my transition to a performing career after my dancing days. She wondered how this new work had affected the pursuit of skills in being more self-aware, present, and real, which I had begun pursuing at the same time. I share my response to her so that you too may begin to wonder about any patterns you have been carrying and reenacting unknowingly. In being more aware, you can bring into your own awareness a new view.

...And then there were all of those TV commercials and ads with animals and children, and the crazy glamour of shooting summer ads in winter, such as wearing strappy gowns and swimsuits out-doors in frigid temperatures. And sometimes it even involved getting into the water.

I remember once posing for a regional magazine cover of a fine dining issue. The male model and I were reclining in a dinghy at the Pacific shoreline in evening attire while the photographer was high on a ladder in his down parka, hat, and gloves shooting from above. The art director was holding the rope so our boat wouldn't wash away in the waves breaking around us, which were filling our boat and splashing us with icy water. My toes were literally blue by the end of that January shoot, but because I was so numb, I wasn't aware of how serious the situation had become.

I also endured winter ads shot in summer, such as the fur coat ad where my makeup was melting off by the pound as the stylist stood by, re-applying color as fast as she could. I nearly passed out. But let's not forget the commercials, sitcoms, and movies where I was involved in dangerous stunts, such as being swung from a man's arms out over the edge of a craggy cliff along the scenic California coast—muddy, steep, rocky, and slick on that memorable rainy day.

This was for a wine commercial. Hmm. . .is the message saying that if one drinks, they do stupid things?

And there were other precarious balancing acts, as when for an Italian calendar I had to sit on a bicycle in a white bikini on a two-foot by four-foot platform in the middle of a killer whale tank during a live performance, while the orca whale and a team of obedient dolphins swam high speed in circles around me, creating rolling waves as they jumped through a ring of fire. Under due duress, I actually was able to stay on the bike, which I believe was just as entertaining for the audience. Is she going to get dumped? Further, let's factor in the stress of my concern for animal rights. For them I cried, and also for myself when realizing I too was just a piece of meat for others' entertainment, to my sheer humiliation clad in embarrassing apparel in a vulnerable situation.

Then there was the high-speed chase scene for a TV series, where I was seated in a mocked-up restaurant on a dock as a car in flight screamed past, blowing my skirt aside on its mad roar off the pier and into the water a few feet from our table. I was the beauty shot closest to the event. Which brings me to the time that I stepped out of an uptown classy hotel as the doors, complete with doormen, swung open wide. A stiletto-toed figure with eyes cast downward beneath a wide-brimmed black hat, I descended the curb into the street as a taxi spinning out of a donut screeched to an abrupt stop within inches of my toes. All this was shot to my perfectly timed arrival, while the doorman opened the cab door and I, unaffected, slid into my motorized yellow carriage on its way to the morgue—for a life insurance commercial. Ah yes, risking my life to sell others life!

There were many more years of such experiences, yet the more grounded in reality I became, due to my self-growth, reconnection, and spiritual integration, the more I began to recognize that this was how it looks when someone is split. Each incident seemed like a separate, disconnected experience, but a theme prevailed throughout and wasn't being addressed. It wasn't until my skills of witnessing and embodiment became more developed that I awoke to the reality that I was being placed in dangerous situations without consent. Nine years into that fifteen-year career, I finally had the wherewithal to speak up and advocate for myself. I shared these incidents with my agent, Jimmy Grimme; he flipped and confronted the ad agencies and clients, arranging for retroactive hazard pay. As the years went on, I began refusing to participate in certain ads, and eventually this chapter of my life needed to end. It was, put simply, a replay of my early childhood trauma pattern.

Functioning From Fear

When we function from fear, and especially from a chronic freeze response, our brains are not thinking clearly. We become much like football players and boxers, for instance, who are rewarded with higher pay the more they endanger their lives. We don't yet realize we have a choice and often are not aware of the full impact of what we are doing and why, or we are heedless and just don't care. A numb brain or a dumb brain, either way healing requires that we disengage from the driving force of the pattern, healing comes when we understand what drives our choice.

I am not implying that all athletes and performers suffer in this way. This was my personal experience, and I know others who used the vehicle of danger to embrace the empirical truth and learn to trust, value, and claim their life.

To say "no" to a habituated pattern means death to something we once valued in our subconscious. Therefore, we must purposefully unlearn a defense mechanism we previously have relied upon. In other words, because we were overpowered or disempowered at some point, it was scary enough that we feared for our life. The freezing response was one way our primitive brain protected us. Like a cat with a mouse, the mouse will freeze and play dead, waiting for the cat to go away so it can run to safety. Likewise, after human trauma, the primitive brain signals that our natural aliveness is dangerous. Those who have encountered tormenting experiences find it difficult to live authentically in the fluid movement of being. Every time the nervous system lets go, relaxes, and involuntarily moves into the flow, fear arises. Yet, we erringly can push the edge just to feel alive, only to shut down once again.

This is the edge we need to titrate in growing a new sense of safety. It is fundamental just to feel safe being in our own skin. And it needs to grow naturally, organically, and gently as with a newborn, or we will likely freak out again. What appears to a healthy person as obvious danger and to be avoided is to a person with trauma structure a nonexistent threat, or an incessant paranoia judging by one's learned frame of reference.[5] In great compassion, having learned from my own life, I empathize with those unaware of an easier way. Until they free themselves, their lives will be fraught with one survival situation after another, replaying the unnecessary trance of traumatic events.

When the five instruments of knowledge stand still together with the mind, and when the intellect does not move, that is called the highest state.

—— Katha-Upanishad: 10, SixthValli[1]

Chapter 7

Trust and Truth

To know the difference between a still mind and the freeze state requires depths of discernment. As the numbing freeze of fear thaws, it can feel like a team of trained horses gone wild while still shackled within the confines of our body. An immense power rises and thrusts to free itself, threatening to derail uncontrollable madness. All the senses are heightened, flooding our system with feelings of overwhelm, and powerlessness. There appears to be no way out.

In this case, single-pointed awareness is needed to provide safe ground, all-be-it grounded groundlessness, amidst the momentum of the runaway charge in the body. Mastering this paradox brings many rewards. Connecting the dots, by bridging basic reality through recognizing the trance of our story and the meaning we give it brings with it great benefits.

As expressed in the Upanishads quote on the previous page, the five instruments of knowledge are our five sense organs––from the gross lesser- developed, purely physical senses to the most subtly refined perceptual sense organs of our soul. Evolving the rudimentary sensory action of the body's impulse to withdraw, fight, or run in a mindful way asks us to be present without acting it out in order that we can successfully reconnect what became disconnected. However, this capacity needs to be developed.

To tolerate such charge usually is not possible in the beginning. It is too intense to be with. Therefore, there are many helpful modalities to assist us along the different stages on our path. First is defensiveness and denial, and then comes the cathartic stage. As the pressure lessons, we can move into more contained forms to develop healthier boundaries and a more integrated, mature self.[2] In the remainder of this chapter, I will walk you through one of my experiences offering you a particular view.

Doubting Our Feelings

...We all have, at one time or another, doubted our feelings, giving ourselves instead to confusion of the mind: Is this true or not? How do I know? What should I trust––what I see, what I am told, what I feel? We look to others for answers, mistrusting our own intuition, sometimes even constructing elaborate stories to justify our decisions. And then there are those few who have no question or doubt as to what is true or false.

It was not so easy for me. A history of complex circumstances threw me into a hurricane of self-doubt, and for decades I struggled with unraveling, discerning, and learning how to trust the truth. What made a difference was that along the way, I began to notice subtle, and sometimes not so subtle, signals that peeked through the morass of confusion. In-between spaces of breath, I heard whispers calling my attention.[3]

At first, I was surprised and put such experiences into a category of special, separate, all by itself. It didn't dawn on me that these invitations could possibly initiate an ongoing way of living because I had cemented right, wrong, good, and bad into a self-created barricade to keep out the world. But I had unwittingly entrapped myself in a false citadel of self-inflicted misery to which only I possessed the key. Thus, I had ensured a fail-proof defense against any chance of letting go. Gripped by my own will in this pseudo protection, I let no one in, and if they did break in, I would just be sitting there—–numb. Although shielded against situations in which I felt God had failed me, at the same time I desperately longed for a home like heaven where I could rest my head and be held.

Little by little, I began to see that the demons were no longer out there but within my own paranoid thinking, which continued to terrorize me and keep my true self at bay. Letting go of control, which I feared most, was understandably the only means by which the door could open. However, with my history of abuse, to have no control also meant to have no will, and to have no will meant death. I falsely believed that in surrender, I would be overtaken and violated in whatever way the demented perpetrators chose. To shine as me would be claiming that I existed, but early experience had warned that to do so was unsafe. During crisis after crisis, I had been passed from one home to another. In my innocence, I had formed the belief that because of me, others were suffering, and so I began withdrawing, trying not to cause others trouble. As I grew older, my forgotten self became so hidden that I no longer knew how to find her.

When I turned 21, my stepfather, whom I was led to believe was my real father, told me the truth. The corkscrew mechanism of shutting down instantly released, sending shock waves of energy throughout my entire body. This thrust of power washed loose my long-held repression and, like a geyser, released up through my body, sending a fountain of light streaming out my crown. To say that I felt tremendous relief and an overflowing sense of gratitude is an understatement, for what he gave me in that instant was my life! Nevertheless, it took three years to find my birth dad at a time when court records were sealed. Another ten years would pass before I could piece together all the disconnected fragments of my early years.

Thank God for the support of my stepfather and the encouragement of my teacher Faisal to keep on looking. Had it not been for their constancy of love, I might not be alive today. For example, finding my birth dad occurred at the same time that my dance career collapsed. Everything on every level was at work to dismantle, in a cascading avalanche, what I had thought of as me. This deconstruction process was mind blowing, and the velocity of hurt, rage, and shock railed, rattled, and rocked me to the core. Even though at last I could consciously bring to light the unknowns buried within, the momentum of reality's shrapnel hit hard. My rational mind could understand why decisions had been made to conceal the truth of my past; however, like a fermented fizzy drink shaken until the cap has blown, my condition was messy to say the least.

Over time, as the fallout settled and I grew my capacity to presence more deeply, I met the most devastating emotional sensation of all——my own self-betrayal. This arose from a deep-seated fear of abandonment (based on real experiences) that drove me to extreme, controlled perfectionism and the need to be good. For survival, I instantly obeyed everyone to avoid being rejected. This got me into dangerous situations because I couldn't trust those whom I needed to, and I minded others who were untrustworthy. My choices were made from fears long past, for I had learned to deny the truth and to trust the lie.[4]

I touched into secret places, revealing unconscious self-abandonment, which inadvertently brought me up against blinding rage. Finally, down under everything else was self-hate, cloaked in the obscuration of self-deception and resentment. It was terribly difficult to be with all of that. In such predicaments, a person wants to die. And in flash moments of agony comes the clear understanding of how, in overwhelming desperation, one could easily end life––the only choice being whether a quick death or a slow execution. How does one sit on this fierce edge with discriminating wisdom? It's a huge force to contend with and requires immense skills of objectivity and discernment while in the upheaval of the tornado––until one reaches its calm center.

Getting the Support We Need

Shortly before all of this happened, I had the good fortune to be working with Dr. Joan Kenly, who had developed Voice Power, a series of breathing and sound techniques to embody what she called the whole-body voice. It was during those sessions with Joan that I started quaking. My high-pitched, choked voice was dropping deeper into my body, opening the diaphragm, belly, and perineum and driving up deep-seated emotions. Finally, I came to her expressing that every time I practiced, I was being flooded with emotions I didn't understand. These were out of proportion to anything else that was going on at the time.

It was then that Dr. Kenly gave me the names of Faisal Muqaddam and Hameed Ali (aka A. H. Almaas), co-creators of the Diamond Approach. I felt an undeniable knowing that I needed to enter that deep body of knowledge, and so I began pearl diving lessons in retrieving my essential identity. I started working with Faisal in 1979 and in 1981 began groups with Hameed. Their work became the pivotal foundation of my personal growth. And so I was held in a gracious network of

Joan, Faisal, and Hameed, who intercepted and redirected my path of self-destruction.

Over and over, I was brought face to face with the realization that

The only way around this pain was through it.

I would have to relinquish my resistance and surrender to the fearful feelings of being out of control without acting them out. This required me to be present and sit with my discomfort by breathing it through, allowing the discharge––the shaking, trembling, icy cold feeling on fire while releasing the fear, shock, rage, and shame, layer after layer after layer, until I had reached the essential medicine reconnecting me with my soul. This was a process that spanned many years.

Giving Up the Struggle

When contemplating giving up the struggle to go beyond my defensive reactions, I heard my young son say, "Mom, you can't say 'surrender.' That's like asking the troops to step down and give up their firearms. It would be dangerous and humiliating." He had called the situation exactly. From the viewpoint of the personal "I," surrender activates a feeling of extreme vulnerability and not being safe, exposing feelings of inadequacy, helplessness, shame, and the unknown. And the unknown, when viewed from a fear perspective, activates the primitive survival response of flight, fight, or freeze. So here we go 'round the mulberry bush, unless we make new choices to renegotiate action other than that of pattern, courageously creating new pathways from which we can self-actualize.

When you catch yourself in the act of avoidance and meet what's really here, right now, this moment, just pause and drop whatever you're doing. You may even hear the gears colliding in your head! All those in-ner voices going off are trying to explain your behavior, blame another, or complain in protest. Here in the now is the only opportunity to meet the pure experience without labeling it right or wrong, good or bad. Otherwise, one just continues to perpetuate a victim identity disguised as the weakling, the unseen, unheard, unwanted, unintelligent, and so on. That's when it's time to get real, to take a stand for the truth, to say no in a conscious way. No more explaining, blaming, and shaming, which are clever tactics to avoid being present, to avoid what is really here——and what may be under even that.

Take pause in the urge to jump out of your skin, and instead get under the skin of any deficient identification. In moments of clarity, expose whatever you have been enacting. Go beneath your defenses to reveal the tenderness of underlying vulnerability. Welcome it with the love you feel toward that "little one" who is so wounded. Be as-sured that whatever you didn't have mirrored back as a child is pre-cisely what you need. And with the pure innocence of an open heart, allow whatever comes up to expose itself in your generous embrace. By opening to this chasm, whatever has been lacking is supplied by the true, essential quality. Thus, we travel from there to here, and here is home——whole, safe, loving, and secure with Self, in our Self, integrated.

Little by little, I was able to allow more sensation and perception into my field of awareness and really be with myself. Even so, it was not comfortable because my patterned grip of control constantly chal-lenged all efforts to be present. My body sent alarming messages that, if it relaxed even a bit, surely my world and everything I knew would fall away. At the edge and ready for flight, I was still captive of the "I" that perceived it was holding the universe together.

It was a lot easier to stay busy than be caught in a moment of emptiness with the terrain of unease packed around it. When living in hyper vigilance, we can't access the full truth. We are in a state of heightened sensitivity, receiving limited information about something long past that we continue to project onto our current situation. Yet if we pause long enough with the in-between of mind (our beliefs) and matter (body sensations), we can interrupt the momentum of our never-ending story of personal history. His-story and her-story want us to believe "I'm this way because…." This is like saying, "I am powerless and incapable of change." If you check, you may discover a sense of smallness under the story that indulges a false identity. The truth is that your essence is all about creation, fluidity, spontaneity, and aliveness——a continuum of co-creation with Source energy with nothing small or diminished about it.

Developing Capacity

As I began developing my capacity for resting in, I could welcome the arising of new beliefs. I was growing an ability to be a witness as well as increasing my tolerance to actually feel. More and more I could stay with the movement of sensation as the energetic charge in my body increased and then released, circulating more naturally.[5] I was cultivating more fluidity of movement and potency of being. My breath was freer, and I felt more at peace. Finally, for the first time in my life, I could relax and was no longer waking up in the morning with my fists clenched and fingernails impressed in my palms. In trusting myself to be here, I was also learning that

All avoidance is avoiding the void.

And the void is nothing more than space. But when mental, emotional, or instinctual centers are separately driving ego-based choices, it becomes scary to open up. The void exposes any susceptibility we may have, for there is nowhere to hide. We imagine that we need to figure it out alone, which exposes even more vulnerability. Because the ego can't "do" what Source "is", because we don't yet trust that our soul, our divine guidance, already has what we need. What's scary for the ego is that we must open to the unknown quality of space in order to receive it. At first, the chasm of space is scary, vacuous, and empty, but eventually we learn to trust and experience it as deeply intimate. Space brings a feeling of friendliness, buoyancy, peace, and calm; it brings us back home to ourselves.

Patience is the key; space is the doorway; love is the medicine.

From out of the darkness, Light appears––the star, our personal point of light, our true essential divine identity––and in realizing the truth of who we are, we no longer feel separation, but become whole. This edge requires dedicated patience, practice, and skill. As a word of caution, let me remark that in the beginning, this path is best not traversed alone. We do not yet have the discernment to detect our whereabouts and, therefore, could instead reinforce the ego's separation panic. Yet, we can manage certain little steps on our own. One is to note that in every moment––no matter what we think, say, or do––we have an opportunity to check in with our inner barometer of truth. I discovered this accidentally one day after a spontaneous, fundamental shift. Instantly, I saw how easy it was. In fact, it was so simple that the more I embraced this process, the freer and happier I became. I was so grateful for such a reliable container from which to access deeper learning. In chapter 9, I share this discovery so that you too can learn how to access your own barometer of truth.

Surah al-Tariq (The Night Visitant)
In the name of God,
Most Gracious, Most Merciful.

By the Sky
And the Night-Visitant
[Therein]——

And, what will explain to thee
What the Night-Visitant is?

[It is] the Star
Of piercing brightness——

There is no soul but has
A protector over it.

Now let man but think
From what he is created!

He is created from
A drop emitted. . . .

—— Qur'an (Surah LXXXVI), translation
by Abdullah Yusuf Al[1]

Chapter 8

Trauma and Spirituality

This verse from the Qur'an reveals that it is within the vast, dark night sky that our true identity can be found. The "star of piercing brightness" eternally illuminates our soul, which is the cloak protecting this most hidden essential Self. This soul is but a drop within the ocean of All-ness. The paradox is that while the soul is the pearly drop housing this bright star, the star is of a much larger field of Light protecting the collective of individuated souls. When learning to recognize, value, and embody our authentic nature, it is important to develop the capacity of discernment between the personality of the learned egoistic "I" and the soul's essential "I."[2]

The "I" of our ego structure is known as the storyteller. It spins the narrative that sets up parameters of selfhood, telling us who we are and from whence we have come. Our stories also act as a reference point that supplies a sense of belonging. When we peer beyond the superficial story, we can grow through deeper self-reflection. By being present and allowing full awareness, our story brings insight to light the way.

Although the telling of our story is a learning tool, we must use caution lest we are swept away in the compulsive momentum of automatic, repetitive recitation. A static tale is devoid of life, stuck in the groove of historical limitation. The more we act out in this way, the more we reinforce an addiction to the same false identity. And if we tell ourselves a scary story, we are in fact being re-traumatized at every delivery, providing little room for growth or change.

Compulsive storytelling is a way to avoid going deeper within, where we may feel the vulnerability of the unknown or see what is hidden in the dark. In these depths, at first we are blind, as though a veil were separating us from the basic truth of reality. The more we might try to control our experience, however, the bigger the chasm we create. In turn, there is more tension, more critical perfection that arises, attempting to keep us from falling and dissolving into the abyss of an undifferentiated self.[3] This is the most wrenching phase of our return home to our native land—wholeness. We feel caught in the madness of limited mind, alienating us from our very light. This is indeed the dark night of the soul.

Embodying Spaciousness

The previous chapter describes an edgy issue concerning one's relationship to space perceived from a trauma perspective. Embodied spaciousness is required to tap the spiritual realm of consciousness and our intrinsic *divine spark* of brilliance. Some traumatic events, such as a near death experience, can induce enlightened states, but more than likely such out-of-body experiences will not be easy to maintain. A more extended spiritual connection can be had through the ongoing rigor of embodied practices, including meditation and contemplation, sacred sexuality, martial arts, chanting, and yoga. Likewise, somatic and psycho-spiritual therapies are helpful in this regard. The constancy of a practice helps to lay down new pathways and gifts of euphoria in gentler, more sustainable ways.

What all ecstasies share in common is the *timeless now,* which often brings on an overwhelming sense of mystic transcendence. As a result, we may have feelings of pleasure, releasing and flooding the system with involuntary movements and washings of selfless love. An ebbing and flowing sweetness wafting around us like a soft sad-full, glad-full joy accompanies this organic infusion. We embody a kind of *amrita,* the nectar of immortality, which fosters whole body-soul union. The sweet sadness of homecoming and the joyous appreciation of longed-for re-union lead us to cherish our arrival. Over time, this state becomes ordinary and the secretions more subtle.

For the embodied person, spiritual awakening adds a substantive potency to the cultivation of being. Spending time in states of bliss enhances the connection with one's preciousness, offering support to live more fully and authentically in the world. The traumatized individual, however, can become frightened and resist feeling aliveness in the body when seeking enlightenment. Because he or she disconnects from body sensations when the pain of trauma becomes too much, the individual splits off from the physical and goes directly to Source awareness.

This remains a huge issue for persons with posttraumatic stress disorder who awaken spiritually yet are not embodied. It can wreak havoc in their lives because the aliveness felt during *awakening* means to their unconscious the same thing as signaled by trauma.[4] Thus, there is a feeling of flightiness, an anxiety that doesn't land. For example, in my younger days, having experienced numerous otherworldly enchantments, I came to believe that the only way to contact that realm was to rise above my body. This tactic only reinforced my fear that it wasn't safe to be here.

In his book *Waking the Tiger*, Peter Levine speaks about traumatic symptoms as not being caused by the event itself but rather the loosened residue of frozen energy in our nervous system. Any time we cannot complete an act of self-protection, all the overwhelmed charge of that energy stays trapped in the body. This creates freezing, bracing, or a state of immobility. In Kathy Kain's trauma bodywork course, we addressed this mechanism in a number of ways. One that opened my eyes was noticing the bracing of a client with no significant trauma that she was aware of.

Later, she discovered that she had swallowed a poison of some kind when very young. While I was working with her, she remembered this as well as having her stomach pumped, which explained why the fluids in her body were operating subliminally. Her body intelligence, still frozen in the old trauma pattern, was still attempting not to spread the toxic chemical. Unconscious of what lay below the surface, she suffered an ongoing hassle because her body didn't respond to anything when she tried to lose weight. She ended up hating her body, which was actually still trying to save her life. Because of this stagnation, her body was in a chronic state of stress-induced inflammation. Her adrenal glands were on overload, exhibiting as frozen on the inside and sluggish on the outside––heavy, lethargic, and depressed. Her energy reserve was forever being tapped, like a racecar's stuck in full throttle while pinned against a wall.

Titrating the Charge

With all forms of trauma, titration is necessary when helping the person or oneself to trust that it is safe to be here, to feel alive in the body again. Titration is a particular technique that supports self-regulation and allows incremental release of the pressurized charge held in the body without overwhelming it. Researcher and clinician Dr. Bessel van der Kolt states that people remember trauma through sensation. When presencing in the body, the challenge is to deal with tremendous emotion (such as fear, horror, or rage) that brings up immense sensations. Or perhaps, the person must recognize lack of ability to be in touch with any emotion or sensation at all. Most important in healing the effects of trauma is to develop a capacity to feel the sensation of the emotion and be willing to meet the charge that is manifesting here——while at the same time, not to push through it so the body feels safe as we learn to trust.

At this point, titration can be most effective. In the beginning, it is recommended to do the work with someone who is skilled. Patience is necessary to keep pace with regulating the charge in the body. It needs to be supported so that the process of discharging any unwanted pent-up energy can be slowed down. With it will come involuntary pressure or movement, such as energy waves in the form of shaking, quivering, jerking, or kicking. These are safely discharging the effects of trauma and relieving chronic stress. The breath can become challenged at this edge,[5] so the four-by-four Resourcing Trauma Breath exercise in chapter 5 is most beneficial. Just concentrate on slow breaths and a pause in-between in equal timing.

Here, what has been expressed as overwhelming emotion such as fear shifts, opening to a gentle sense of calm. This is the calm of being, and being is love. Over time we learn that this is a love we can trust; it will neither abandon nor harm us. Eventually, we also discover that love has always been available, and it has been we ourselves who have rejected, hidden, or forsaken it.

Reflecting on the Effects of Trauma

As I reflect upon the personal history of clients and students from the last twenty years, I realize that approximately 85% have had damaging, lasting effects due to emotional and physical trauma after having grown up in homes with alcoholism, drug abuse, mental health issues, rape, bullying, divorce, loss, or death of family members. Of those, nearly 30% also have endured satanic ritual abuse, abduction, extreme neglect, violence, or life-threatening accidents or disease. No wonder the stress levels in our society are increasing as people find it more and more difficult to function. Whether we harbor ill feelings internally or act them out, the consequences equal a death sentence. This intensity of imploded energy drains our vitality, leaving us vulnerable to apathy and hostility. No wonder the overuse of caffeine and sugar are at an all-time high as we grasp false stimulation just to get by.

Put simply, trauma occurs when we become overwhelmed and are unable to successfully discharge the flooding energy, thus impacting our lives in detrimental ways. If not dealt with, this charge can lead to chronic pain, low self-esteem, depression, self-abuse, bullying, addiction, suicide, and murder. Trauma can be physical, psychological, or emotional; but whatever the original impetus, eventually all three systems are affected. This is how posttraumatic stress (PSTD) leaves its mark and why it is vital that we seek proper treatment.

It may take a network of skilled practitioners to usher our return to balance. Depending on what is being addressed, resources can vary widely. Beneficial responses include psychotherapy, grief counseling, behavioral or cognitive behavioral therapy (CBT), short-term medication to break the stress cycle, somatic experiencing (SE) work, attachment disorder therapy, or other modalities that deal with trauma, such as eye movement desensitization, reprocessing (EMDR), and so on. Gentle hands-on methods, such as touch trauma resolution, cranial work, ortho-bionomy, and matrix repatterning, can greatly benefit the nervous system to help release the charge so the body can rest. In addition, the simple movements taught in brain gym, brain dance, and zapchen somatics can help balance the right and left hemispheres of the brain. Writing to yourself is empowering, as are breathwork, chanting, dance therapy, art therapy, yoga and psycho-drama, sound nutrition, and a spiritual practice.

The Paralyzing Inability to Self-Protect

…As I grew older, the cascading effect of early childhood trauma lent itself to a paralyzing inability to say "no," run away, or tell my parents what had happened. Referred to as a thwarted defense mechanism, this pattern left me unable to protect myself. As a result, I was molested and raped by different neighbors on several occasions throughout my childhood. The tricky part came years later when I had embodied enlightenment experiences. The all-consuming Light shone on where I had split off consciousness, after which countless buried instances of separation rose to the surface asking for mercy. I had to go through the entire grieving process for my lost innocence and feeling of aloneness. In turn, I had to forgive in order to melt into and through any place that was still reactive—otherwise it would not be forgiven. I needed self-forgiveness, to forgive others and God, as well as to ask for forgiveness. All these steps are necessary to heal and return to a trustworthy sense of wholeness.

Acts of atonement *reveal* the Light, yet to *receive* the Light is to be penetrated by the Light. If the issue is around sexuality, the unconscious will translate this Light as being penetrated by God. As a result, any shame about our sexuality will surface instantly. We will meet our

primitive, wild, instinctual nature when allowing the internal movement of this energy. All kinds of beliefs will be exposed, even those we
do not suspect that we carry. As the basement clears, this energy tran-
scends to give us more awareness.

Dealing With Stress

Trauma also has a dire effect on our endocrine system, especially the
adrenal glands, the key system for dealing with stress (which at its root
is fear) When the adrenals are taxed, all manner of issues arise. One
overlooked factor in dealing with trauma is the benefit of nutrition. In
his book *The Body Shape Diet*, nutritionist and chemist Dr. Cass Ingram
brilliantly outlines a map of the endocrine system and its functions.
There are twelve glands in the system, each pared with a specific organ
to regulate. Dr. Ingram offers a detailed test to find out a person's endocrine body type and subtype. He also gives details about what foods best
support metabolism of the glandular functions for the different body
types. I highly recommend that everyone become acquainted with this
groundbreaking research.

Dr. Ingram's investigation into scientific research sheds light on the
optimal metabolizing effects of foods for each person. As an adrenal
type, I was eating in a way that was harming my body and increasing
my stress and fatigue. The macrobiotic diet I had chosen consisted primarily of vegetables and grains, but no flesh, dairy, or eggs. I had grown
increasingly more nervous and fatigued. When I reduced the amount of
veggies and grains and included more protein, fruits, nuts, and seeds, I
became more relaxed and energized. A different endocrine body type,
however, would actually thrive on the very foods not suited for me.
Likewise, metabolism can be affected by trauma, either by increasing or
decreasing metabolic function, resulting in weight gain or weight loss,

for example. So both the adrenal glands and the thyroid gland can be greatly challenged by imbalances caused by trauma.

Dr. Ingram goes on to say that adrenal types are highly stressed by overstimulation, such as too much energy from chaos, noise, fluorescent lights, and other unwelcome ambient situations. Many of these individuals are extremely psychic and diversely affected by the psychic fields of others. Scientific studies show their sensitivity to smells may be 1,000 to 100,000 times greater than normal.[6] This state will return to balance once they regulate their glandular function through proper diet and wise choices. But they will always be more sensitive than others. These types can become easily exhausted from too much stimulation or stress. Emotional entanglements, especially anger, frustration, and worry, are not only detrimental but also likely to perpetuate feelings of powerlessness, hopelessness, and victimization, contributing to a downward spiral in health. The adrenal glands are vital to life and when impaired can cause imminent wasting disease and death. A calming, serene, and rejuvenating environment is both lifesaving and essential for this person's sense of well-being.

When we get caught in the confusion of not knowing what we need, a simple, quick, and easy tool can go a long way. The truth or lies exercise, Divining the Truth, in chapter 9 is a wonderful resource to begin building a sense of trust in yourself for making new choices in claiming what is most beneficial to you, from you. It helps to align your personal will with divine will, integrating the self of your ego structure with the essential Self, the soul's true nature. It offers an instantaneous biofeedback response to help create more peace and ease in your life. Adrenal types tend to overthink their options and then worry about choices they have made. This simple exercise will help you drop under any mental compulsion. You will learn to stop and drop into the moment, sensing the immediacy of *what is* and *always was* here to support us! Are you ready to venture in a new way?

Section Three

Intuition and Truth

black
dark, shadows
swirling, darkening
shady, murky, light, lantern
lightning, brightening
color, bright
white

—— Tarik Muqaddam, 9 years old[1]

Chapter 9

Divining the Truth

The year was 1986.

Solace rapt in stillness ascending the blackened stairwell ends; the silence is shattered as the accuser shouts, "Turn on the lights, idiot, before you fall."

At once contracted, darkness darkening, my mind spinning with thoughts of incrimination... shrinking, it hits me! Suspended in a pregnant pause. . .it suddenly dawns on me: I have a choice. In a flight of insight, my brilliance connects to a wondering. "Is what this person saying really true?" Instantly, I become more contracted, asking, "Whose truth is it anyway?"

With nano speed, the response infuses me——my realization lights like a bulb switched on, brightening the hallway in shining light. Astonishment stops me in my tracks. Time stretches everywhere at once as I grok the magnitude of the reality——I have long

participated in diminishing myself. I have been buying into others'
negativity, sickly pleasing to feel wanted. My stomach feels queasy
seeing this truth.

Until this realization, I had been so enmeshed in others' worlds that
I wasn't aware of how I was disempowering myself.[2] Now I could
clearly see that I continuously had sacrificed my self-worth and power by unconsciously joining their belittling of me. I had victimized
myself by flagellating and punishing myself for just being me. I felt
so much delight in recognizing that I had been blaming them for
using me like a doormat when, in fact, it was I who was actually letting myself down.

What a relief. A ton of pressure released when I got that. On this
bright night, I provided some spacious objective clarity when I *"stopped*
and dropped" into the real truth of that momentous moment. By not
reacting and by staying neutral, I interrupted my habituated automatic
response, which would have kept my old story intact. Instead, I chose
not to corroborate the verbal attack, which had brought to light the
unconsciously embedded pattern of my past.[3]

It feels odd to me now to even imagine that I was once this way.
When I consider the immense expenditure of energy invested in maintaining such patterns of habit, the cost is incomprehensible. Yet the effect of trauma can be mighty, whether physical, emotional, or mental. It
is like an energetic hole exhausting our life force. Trauma has a negative,
life-extinguishing energy all its own, fueled by the aftermath of a helpless, hopeless, powerless thwarted defense. Change is not possible until
the readiness comes to see that the deed has already been done: execution by one's own hand. For it is we ourselves who need to see what it is
that we do and choose not to do it.

Excited by my discovery, I continued to test my findings, asking again if this person's statement was in fact about me. Again I contracted and dimmed. Clearly the words felt untrue. So I made a firm reply, saying, "It's not mine." At once I felt an ease, expanded and full. There is a sense of freedom and lightness in one's essential truth. *Truth is easy.* I had not known that before.

Daring to Have a New Experience

By now the ranting of the accuser was rambling on below, fading in the background as I proceeded to another room where I could practice my new-found game of Truth and Lies. There I reviewed the steps I had taken and decided to turn this event into a way to support my continuing growth. As with any research in which one wants to develop a consistent, reliable outcome, I created a baseline consisting of a known truth as well as a known lie to gauge my results. I experimented with a variety of questions, some about which I knew the answer and some I didn't. These I could evaluate at a later date. It was a night to celebrate. By not abandoning myself, I had experienced a new self-trust, and over time my self-confidence grew.[4]

So the question I bring forth is: Do you dare entertain an idea of a new you? Are you willing to let go of what you've outgrown and no longer serves you? Maybe let go a little? Perhaps a lot! Might you like to experiment with this exercise yourself? Go ahead and try it on and maybe, just maybe, you may like it. If not, nothing is lost. So then, ask: What does truth look like? And how does it feel? Ok, I'll share with you what I've discovered, practiced, and taught to hundreds of students over the years.[5]

First, it is important that you arrive at a place that feels as neutral as possible. To do this, open your awareness, witnessing yourself by not getting in the way. Let go of your brain muscle and simply allow it to go along for the ride. For now, it is just a passenger, an observer, and it doesn't need to drive. Imagine the brain as soft as a marshmallow, fluffy and floating in your head!

Let's begin. Start by releasing your jaw. Drop it slightly (about the width of your little finger) so that your back molars are not touching. As you do this, allow your eyes to soften and, like your brain, float in the surrounding fluid. Your throat, chest, belly, hips, knees, hands, and feet soften as well. Next, inhale and allow the belly, diaphragm, and chest to fill like a balloon. As you exhale, your belly returns to neutral, releasing air.

For this exercise to be accurate, you will be asked to notice, and eventually rely on, what arises in the field of your subtle perception. Meanwhile, the scent, taste, texture, sound, and vision of the sensate terrain will be heightened. Now choose a statement that is a known truth and say to yourself something that is a fact, such as your name, age, a food you like, or someone you love. Immediately your body will respond. Don't try to think about it. Sense it. The response is instant.

You may feel a softening, relaxation, or expanding quality. Maybe you sense a brightness, lightness, or freedom of breath. Say the statement of truth to yourself again, and pay attention to the instantaneous response in your body and in your field. Experiment with other statements of truth until your barometer is tuned to give you consistent, reliable information that is unique to you. A variety of responses can represent truth, and you will discover those that are especially right for you. You may sense a subtle glow, openness, or scintillating quality of aliveness, ease, fullness, softness, and so on. But whatever occurs will express an expansive, light feeling that is full of ease.

Next, make a false statement to yourself, something that is an out-and-out lie. Notice what happens. Do you feel yourself withdraw, shrink, or collapse? Is there a sensation that is dull, contracted, or hard? Is there agitation, fogginess, swirling, or nausea? Did your light dim? Maybe you held your breath or it felt tight or stuck.

If you were able to simply be with the truth or the lie without impos-ing a preference or judgment onto your experience, then you may have felt some of these sensations for correctly detecting yes or no. If your experience was instead opposite of what you know, such as contraction in response to the truth statement or expansion in response to the lie statement, then it is possible you were not in neutral. In this case, yes would mean no and no would mean yes, as in what happened to me when I denied my truth.

Letting Go of Attachment

For example, sometimes we are attached to a particular outcome, and this gets in the way of clearly and objectively sensing or seeing. If so, perhaps there is fear or unwillingness to change or be different than the way we have known. It takes time and patience for some of us, while others will get this instantly. Each person is unique and brings her own individual history, orientation, and process. Patterns of trust and mistrust are formed before we learn to speak, and the program of denial may seem normal according to your programmed reality.

My sense of truth became turned around and entangled at a young age, disempowering myself so I wouldn't be rejected. Because much of this survival mechanism was preverbal, it took a long time to decipher. I had to learn how to discern truth and trust myself. Many of you have experienced some variation of this theme. So if your truth is flipped, it is of primary importance to strengthen your muscles of discernment.

Here is a practice that supports and connects you with basic reality, which is beneficial in creating safe, constant ground to establish simple truth. For example, say, "This is the floor," "I feel it support me," "It feels solid." Or squeeze the arm of the chair, saying, "I feel the chair holding me," and so forth, connecting your physicality to what is solid and reliable, something basic that you can trust. This is a time for building structure, to come into the body. It is *not* the appropriate moment to claim, "Nothing is solid because we are only 4% matter, and we're mostly made up of space!" Don't let the head talk the body out of having a grounded experience. Let the nervous system experience safe ground so it can rest into your body, so that the body can feel safe and relax.

This exercise may seem ridiculous, yet for those who were harmed in such a way that the truth got twisted, it is a powerful, grounding jewel. As you practice growing a trusting relationship with yourself, you will, in turn, learn to root in your body in basic truth, emerging with a clear sense of stability. Watch that the mind does not repeat what I did early in my spiritual growth, which was to dismiss and bypass basic reality in search of exalted spiritual experiences. The rebound was big and the fall great because the container had not been developed. Like a pendulum, I swung from one extreme to the other for a very long time. That may happen at a certain stage, but then we integrate and move on. Because of my own structure, this prolonged swing intensified my trauma loop. I didn't land. I was missing the fundamental steps that need to be developed. And the most basic is the humility of coming down to earth.

So truth gets distorted through identifying with the charge (*emotional*), or wanting to control the outcome (*mental*), or simply needing hydration (*physical*). If we are dehydrated, we will get a false reading: false will be true and true will be false. If you get the opposite response to a statement that is a known truth, the first thing is to drink a glass of water. If that doesn't shift, then wet your finger and dip it in sea salt, placing it on your tongue to mineralize yourself. Give it a few minutes to absorb, and then re-test. You may find you need additional water. It is amazing that the more hydrated you are, the more easily you can detect what is true or not. And not all water is hydrating; if it is acidic, our cells won't easily take it in. You can study water research to learn how it communicates. Our bodies are 75%–90% water, depending on the method of measure.

We ourselves are a divining rod of truth. Truth is simple and has nothing on it. There are no edges. Truth is light, free, full, and pure. Truth is alive, loving, and illuminating. Each moment we choose truth marks a new beginning.

We are like imaginal cells, able to manifest fuller potential. By unique design, we have an inborn navigational mechanism that can point either toward or away from truth. This innate barometer operates like the divining rod that dowsers use when witching for water. My grandfather was a dowser. People from all around would call on him to find water on their land so they could dig a well for their orchards, livestock, or home. This was in northern California where the willow and cottonwood trees were plenty and shared a special relationship with water.

On a Dowsing Excursion

I had the opportunity to go on several dowsing excursions with my grandfather. He would begin at the periphery, scoping the land from afar. Then he would bow his head in reverence as he stepped onto the area being surveyed. Next he would find a tree and fashion a tool, picking off a branch just below the joint where an incoming stem divided into two outstretched arms like a giant wishbone. Cleaning away all twigs and leaves, he honed the wood until it was smooth. Then, lightly balancing the two free ends in each hand, he pointed the tip forward and walked about while watching for the branch to move. The closer he got to an underground water source, the more the pull and the faster the rod would rock. If farther away from the source, it would just lie limp. As he returned again toward the prime location, fine-tuning the spot, the rod would become more and more energized until, like the union of magnetically attracting forces, the tip pulled straight down, pointing to the earth. Here is where the men would dig a well; and they always found water. One day, Grandpa handed the divination rod to me, and I walked the land. I felt the vibratory aliveness so strongly that it seemed like holding onto an excited, wiggling bunny. Grandpa said,

This is the miracle of God working through
the living water that is in everything alive.

That brief encounter motivated me to understand our relationship with water, which led to knowing through direct experience the synergy of divine alignment by utilizing life's healing waters in us.

Eventually, my lifelong quest brought me to the subtle energy system of *latifas,* which I learned about from my teacher and, later, husband, Faisal. I studied the sacred medicine of our soul's essence with him for 23 years. In this methodology, a person identified with fear, doubt, or lies finds his essential water drying up. By contrast, a congruent individual anchored in the loving truth is streaming and full, filled with the divine elixir of nutritive fluid——hence the saying, *"My cup runneth over."* So play with this as you notice which thoughts or actions leave you feeling withered and which blossom you. Receiving the latter, you are the water, the divining rod, and the geomancer——all parts unified in the wholeness of the One——a divine holographic matrix, communicating and connecting with everything and everyone.

Now let's review this exercise so that you too may apply it to your daily life, empowering choices that will nourish and grow you.

Divining the Truth

Sit comfortably:
Soften the eyes, unhinge the jaw, rest down in the hips. Feel your thighs and back supported by the chair.

Breathe:
Inhale, expanding the abdomen, diaphragm, and chest. Return to neutral with your exhalation. Rest into the flow of the natural breath.

State a truth:
Say out loud a known truth, something you know for a fact to be true.

Notice:
What sensation do you feel in the body, or energetically? Note that.

State an untruth:
Say out loud a known lie, something you know for a fact to be false. Note that.

Notice:
What sensation do you feel in the body, or energetically? Note that.

> *The Whole Truth, about Truth, is that Truth*
> *is a Whole Experience.*

In the presence of truth all of you expands––all of you eases and feels a lightness spread.

> *What is whole is true, and truth is love––*
> *you being true to the being*
> *you truly are.*

It is important to remember when you say the true-or-false statement that all three centers (head, chest, and belly) respond together. Otherwise, the answer is only a partial truth, thus wishy-washy and unreliable. Here are some tips for success:

* If your three centers do not respond together, adjust your statement until you get a full response one way or the other.
* Truth will be lighter, brighter, open, and expansive. Truth can be scintillating, soft, spacious, and delicate.
* You may experience one or more of these qualities, or something not mentioned that feels really positive, when you access what is true.

*   A lie will be dim, hard, rigid, heavy, or dense. A lie is represented by a contractive, constricted, stuck energy.

These energetic responses are occurring all the time, yet most of us are not even aware of what is happening. As you become more skilled in perceiving these nuances, decision making and trusting yourself will become easier. Ease and flow are essential for well-being. Truth moves toward life; a lie moves away from life.

It is amazing how many of us have worked in jobs and been in relationships where we have denied our true desires. We have learned to compromise ourselves in so many ways on so many levels that we eventually grow insensitive to our misalignment. We have forgotten the love that we truly Be––true alignment with our being. Yet when we wake up and claim for ourselves what is true, strength arises from our very marrow, providing for us the courage to step out into the world anew. The more we learn to trust our truth, the more our confidence grows.

The following is a declaration that a student wrote and shared in class. It celebrates mastery of the ability to trust her truth. As a result, new and exciting opportunities opened, greatly enriching her life.

TRUTH !

Honor your truth!
Listen to your truth!
  Walk your truth!
    Resonate with the ways things are in this truth!
      Your truth is who you really are,
        Living in conscious awareness and authenticity!

It is painful to function in a system that isn't in
truth!
It matters who you are and where you
walk in your truth!
Growth will find you, and you
will know each other!

—— Hazel Gilley

May each one of you be blessed with the freedom that this simple practice can bring. True alignment has transformed my life and the lives of
many of my students. Every time we choose the truth we are choosing
the Light, and the Light guides our Way!

IT'S RIGGED

It's rigged——everything, in your favor.
So there is nothing to worry about.

Is there some position you want,
some office, some acclaim, some award, some con, some lover,
maybe two, maybe three, maybe four——all at once,

maybe a relationship
with
God?

I know there is a goldmine in you; when you find it
the wonderment of the earth's gifts you will lay
aside as naturally as does
a child a
doll.

But, dear, how sweet you look to me kissing the unreal:
comfort, fulfill yourself in any way possible——do that until
you ache, until you ache,

then come to me
again.

—— Julaludin Rumi[1]

Chapter 10

Judgment and Wholeness

The mysterious unknown is a quality of spaciousness that opens us to new possibilities. But often we tell ourselves stories to persuade others to join in our more limited point of view, cutting off opportunities to claim with awareness what we do not yet know.[2] We are thus prone to make judgments that separate us from our integral wholeness, where there is no need to justify anything. I am using the word *judgment* to refer to criticism, self-righteousness, or any other way we create separation. Judgment is not to be confused with discernment, but only the process of making something wrong so the judger, of self or others, can be right. Because judgment is grounded in a deep, unconscious belief of one's own inadequacy, it separates us from our wholeness and truth.

Here's a crazy thought. Judgment is based on a truth we cut off from ourselves but project onto our relationship with another person, situation, or thing. What's brilliant here is that our judgment may be based on fact, but it becomes distorted when we isolate, criticize, or use it to create separation. We often do this so we can hang on to the feeling of having been treated unjustly in life. And then we keep on proving it over and over again. All judgments are projections.

Say for instance you want a monogamous partnership but in the past you experienced betrayal. Someone cheated on you, a parent cheated on the other, or you grew up with ideas about relationships based on others' experience. So now you carry the mantra that "Men aren't faithful," which is a distortion of the masculine principle. Still, you don't understand why it's not working out for you to have a decent relationship. The person you married got drunk and slept with your best friend, and the others you dated never really left their old relationship, and you discovered they've been two timing all along, and the ones in between weren't really interested in pursuing you. So here you are. You haven't connected the dots, remaining unconscious to the pattern you are repeating. Then you use it as proof that men can't be trusted, which further embeds the pattern. To top it off and distract you more, there is a social agreement that compares men to animals, sowing their seeds for the survival of the species. Thus in framing men this way, women carry on with their mistrust of men, and men are hit with a collective unconscious energy that promotes promiscuity.

It's an edgy dance to meet all that energy and yet evolve one's consciousness. We can exchange the idea of men with women or women with men here because it is not as much about gender as about gender identity. In addition, according to the cultural judgment of women, they are weaker and less intelligent, which is a distortion of the feminine principle. This may lead a woman to do whatever it takes to get a man to protect her, even if that means using pregnancy as a trap. Not every unwed woman who gets pregnant is doing this, but such deception splits off the fuller truth, leaving one out of balance and disconnected from wholeness. If the person steps into a relationship that is already grounded in mistrust, no wonder he or she can't understand why it is not working. These examples are gross stereotypes, but sadly they are common even today.

Seeing the Truth

To be with the full truth is to remove our blinders, seeing what we have not been noticing. From this awareness, there really isn't any prejudice. We are simply observing pure facts, basic reality, the whole truth. Open awareness shows us everything from every direction possible––anywhere we've created splitting by making something good or bad, right or wrong. It exposes any place we have created limitation or separation. As we allow ourselves to have this fuller, spacious witnessing experience, we can bring back together the fragmented parts. Thus, we reconnect the chasm, bridging what was compromised in our mind-body relationship.[3] As a result, we get to see the fuller picture. The synapses begin firing again, as when a shaman helps retrieve the lost parts of the soul. Psychology speaks of this as integrating different aspects of personality, science calls it connecting neurological pathways, and spirituality mentions the integration into wholeness.

When we look honestly at what is here and own what's not working in life, without making up stories or excuses and allowing ourselves to see the situation purely as it is, without judgment, we will expose sabotaging thoughts that have created this reality in the first place. Say for instance that you want a car, a house, or a vacation but do not see how it is possible financially. You say, "I want such and such, but I can't afford it because…," and then proceed to defend all the reasons why it can't work, reinforcing the limitation based on past conditioning. What you are doing is repeating what did *not* work and defending why not! You are perpetuating your lack and limited view, and then getting lost in a looping, convoluted pattern.[4] This way you hold on to what's familiar, and what's familiar feels safer than feeling the deficiency of *not knowing*. Once again, you've cut yourself off from any possibility of having what you desire. When you catch yourself in this dilemma, you may want to ask, "The survival fear of this mechanism is motivated to avoid what?"

Take heart in the adage "To change, one must see what is here." Improvement doesn't just happen; we have to show up, make a commitment to ourselves, and be willing and courageous enough to live in a different way, a way we have not yet known.

> *The secret is that if we include everything*
> *we already know, see, and feel,*
> *and also include what we don't know, see, or feel,*
> *allowing both to be fully present in our*
> *awareness without prejudice,*
> *we can then open ourselves up to the spaciousness*
> *of an unknown mysterious reality and*
> *the generous gift it has to offer.*

The pure, expansive nature of spaciousness is unbiased, neutral, and without preference. From here, we can move in several directions simultaneously. We can be with the energy of any contractive thought, pain, or sensation while at the same time including the larger field of unknowing, which is devoid of object or thing. Spaciousness holds these opposites––letting go to the arising presence of the mystery. Everything is possible. We will explore this concept more in the next chapter.

Being With the Energies

The energies of our conditioned patterns act like magnetic generators, drawing us to anything that is of a resonant, matching frequency. It is happening all the time whether we are aware of it or not. But I assure you that once you cultivate a clear understanding of how you are perpetuating limitation, your life will begin to change, and I mean really change. So be willing to consider the question, "Do I really want change?"

There's a joke in my groups that arises year after year about how classes should come with a warning: "Join at your own risk." If you are not open to change, this course is inappropriate. In my groups, nearly all participants will experience a job change, promotion, relationship change, or a residence move in the process of recognizing energy patterns that don't serve their highest good. In some classes, folks have experienced all three changes as they have learned to trust that

What is true comes with ease, and what is not is a struggle.

If you are struggling, look at what is not in alignment with your truth. When you allow objectivity rather than indulging the auto-pattern, you are guided in mysterious ways. You become an instrument of Source, your will aligning with divine will and amplifying the outcome. Eventually your alignment with divine guidance becomes so natural that you know going against it will cause great suffering. Thus, you learn to develop impeccable precision of clarity along with the ability to live with one foot in both worlds––seen and unseen, known and unknown––embodying both your human potential and celestial heritage. You will be tested in all kinds of ways with plenty of opportunity to practice your skills. Over time, your boundaries will be neither wishy-washy nor rigid, but like a deep-rooted tree that is both steadfast and flexible.

In the process of integration, our once painful, deficient self-identity——based on separation that is want to leave us feeling lost, alone,
betrayed, abandoned——matures and grows up. At last, we turn toward
our essential self. In the beginning, one's ego deficiency doesn't trust
anything or anyone, especially not Essence. After fully expressing self in
the past, it may have experienced negative consequences, finding that
total aliveness can be too much, inappropriate, or uncomfortable for
others. Sadly, we then learned to sparkle down so we could feel wanted.

Practicing Constancy

When you practice the simple exercises here, you are developing a ground
of constancy. You will keep showing up for yourself again and again no
matter what, developing what did not mature when you were young.
You are growing up this part, holding your own hand. The witness-self
is the adult, and the deficiency is like a little child that does not know
how to be or what to do, and is so afraid. When your inner adult and
inner child join together, you will have a healthier ego.

But something else really important has been happening all along.
Every time you return to a felt sense of wholeness, you will know this
as your Being. As the ego begins to trust, it is no longer so unconscious
or attached to self-preservation. It lays aside its divisive tactics, stops
creating painful separation, and accepts that there is in fact a reliable
container in which to be held.

This is the returning process in which the ego turns toward the
Beloved, one's essential Self. The head bows to the heart, just as in early
embryonic life when in the womb your crown furled in toward your
sacred heart. Life becomes easeful from the resiliency of this new way

of being, true to your higher Self. Another way to say this is that at first ego doesn't trust essence. Then ego turns toward essence, learning it can be trusted. At last ego rests its head to the heart, embracing essence. Ego and essence are united——an egoless ego. You realize that you are no longer powerless but open, infinitely re-sourced, and able.

In 2002, I got to trust the guidance of my being by making a radical move. I had been living in the Bay Area most of my life, enjoying a private healing arts practice. But I was struggling to stay afloat as a single mom with expenses beyond my means. I had been recently divorced and was coming through years of chronic fatigue. Now I was hitting bottom. The ground I was attempting to build was dissolving from under my feet faster than I could keep up. Living in a chronic state of exhaustion, I knew it was time to follow the guidance I had received a decade before: to leave the Bay Area. All previous attempts had fallen through for reasons seemingly out of my control. Under it all, however, I had become aware of how vulnerable it would feel to leave my support system of healers, family, and friends as well as the financial support of my work. I was haunted by the impending fear that I would not have enough energy both to move and restart my business.

Facing the Truth

But the real truth was that I was afraid to leave what I thought of as security. But why did a move feel so incredibly paralyzing? What was it that really kept me from going forward? Eventually, I had to drop down into myself even more to see that my terror was related to my early loss of home after home, along with the loss of one parent and then the other. Remembering this brought up the deep-seated false identity of not belonging anywhere. So I unconsciously grasped fiercely to what I already had. In that "aha" moment, I got it. It was now easy to see.

Looking back, I realize how the fear of enduring more unbearable pain pre-sabotaged my every attempt to move. Once I recognized what I had so deeply hidden, exposed it, and held it with love, I felt the courage to take the necessary steps. With that recognition, I felt an inner strength, an integral alignment in a wholly connected way. No longer was I caught in the undertow of an unconscious struggle, for the internal conflict had been brought to light. From the perspective of wholeness, I held no doubt about the truth. The idea of the need for change came with the clear vision that it was time to actualize a move.

For two years I had explored hamlets around the greater Bay Area, Southern California, Nevada, and even Portland, but nothing took hold. Then I decided to go on a five-day scouting trip, this time asking Divine Guidance to direct my search. I resolved to drive only in the direction in which my whole being remained open. I was drawn, like a magnetic force pulling my entirety northward, out of California, through Oregon, and then up to Washington, landing in the rainiest state on our continent. My mind could not wrap itself around what was happening. I, the sun worshipper, was heading into the third-largest rainforest on our planet. It did not compute. Yet the alignment to what was whole and true was a force I couldn't deny. So bowing to the Grace of what was bigger than myself, rather than trying to manipulate it to please my preference of going south, I landed on Cooper Point in Olympia, Washington.

Suddenly, my entire pituitary axis ignited.[4] It was like a starburst exploding from my head, shooting down through my body and into the earth, then out my crown and into the universe in every direction at once. I blurted out loud, "I'm home!" Was I crazy, or what?

I called my dear friend in California and shared the news, after which he said, "Congratulations! Now pick up a newspaper and look for a house!" A half hour later, I pulled off the road into a driveway to read the paper, found a listing, and called the realtor. Sitting in that driveway, little did I know how Divine synchronicity was steadily at work.

Two weeks later, after my return trip to California, my friend and I flew up and met the realtor I had previously called. As the agent was showing us houses, he asked if we would mind stopping by his home nearby so he could drop off something. Lo and behold, we pulled into the very same driveway from which I had first called him two weeks earlier. Without knowing a thing, I had landed in exactly the spot where I would be wanting to go.[5]

> *Ask and it shall be given you,*
> *seek, and you will find,*
> *knock, and it will be opened to you.*

— Jesus, Matthew 7:7, Aramaic Bible

When you identify with the limitation of scarcity consciousness, you will get more of that. If you say, "I don't have enough money," for example, the universe (uni-verse, your very own logos, the words you think and say) will create the lack you are espousing. If you are telling yourself you don't have enough money, the unconscious obeys the command and will sabotage any attempt to have money. Change what you tell yourself and the Self will respond in kind! Because if you are willing to drop your old story, ask an open-ended question, and receive the genius of Divine Will, the possibilities are infinite.[6]

Asking doesn't mean saying, "I want, I want, I want."
Asking is the act of spacious open attraction.
It is surrendering to receive the fluid flow
of being and embodying the abundance.[7]

Here's a secret about the mechanism of *Will*. If there is tension, don't trust it. What? But that's not what we're taught. We're encouraged to have a strong will and to enforce our will. So how is that working for you? Is it opening doors of opportunity and greeting you with open arms? I don't think so. Is it easeful and rewarding? Really? Surrendering your will is having the humility that you can't do it alone.

True Will is the act of surrendering your personal will to Divine Will, as I discovered when I was about to move. For two years, I tried looking here, there, and everywhere for places I thought I wanted to move. That involved so many considerations and a lot of effort, and my search did not go so well. Yet when I let go of the effort, surrendered my will, and trusted the guidance of Source, it all changed. The entire move flowed with a synchronicity I couldn't have planned if I had tried. That move proved to be beneficial beyond anything I had imagined. My health improved and a community grew unlike any I had experienced in all my years of living in the Bay Area. It became a dream come true.

WILD FORCES

There are beautiful wild forces within us.

Let them turn the mill inside
and fill
sacks

that feed even
heaven.

—— St. Francis of Assisi[1]

Chapter 11

Energetics of Balance

As long as we are busy exerting our willpower, we are not open to receive what the divine has to gift us. Effort is a one-way road, but abundance is a reciprocal movement that is all-inclusive.

As within, so without; as above, so below.

—Hermes Trismegistus, *The Emerald Tablets*

When we try too hard, we create tension. Tension causes stuckness, which interferes with our feeling of wholeness, the integrity of balance. If we presence the tension, it is perceived as some kind of energetic separation. Energetic separation can be caused when acting judgmentally. Judgment arises sometimes in the most unlikely situations, such as in the following narrative that arose during a student's morning walk. Not only did it expose the separation that was created but also what such thoughts could grow.

Cows and... I just got it! Those cows in that pasture over there, I don't relate to them. They are literally "the other." However, these cows...my friends, right here...I know them intimately. But seriously, are those cows any different from these cows? Nope. World peace will happen as soon as we take down the fences and unite these and those. It's just a vowel from now. These and those—just one letter away. One letter makes all the difference.

—— Joanne Cooper, student[2]

It is brilliant to notice, energetically, the effect that separation has on us. Earlier we got to see with the Truth or Lies exercise how a truth brought fullness and a lie contracted. Next we will include in our awareness four polarities of movement and any expansive and contractive forces that we can detect. Let's explore the energetics of how we create separation yet don't realize it. This is going on all the time unbeknown to us until we dial in our perceptual sensitivity enough to detect the profound effect we are creating erroneously. Once conscious, we will instantaneously and effortlessly create for ourselves a new and empowering experience.

This is a simple exercise that will help you notice where awareness is and is not. This easy, practical tool can be applied anywhere, anytime. You don't have to delve into the complexity of issues. What you will learn is how to effortlessly return again and again to a sense of balance and wholeness. This is something you can do on your own. And then when you do attend to the bigger work, such as exploring issues of concern, you will have already laid down the beneficial groundwork of orientation.

Presencing Polarities

With this exercise you will be presencing four polarities of movement: *Up and Down, Forward and Back, Side to Side, In and Out.* Start by sitting in a chair, feet flat on the ground, or you can stand. If you choose to stand, be sure that the backs of the knees and the fronts of the ankle are soft and slightly released. With each direction, note the dominant energy present.

Let's begin with up and down. Is the energy more concentrated in the upper body or lower body? When you check in, where do you sense it first? I am asking you to notice where the energy is most concentrated, more stuck, whatever it is that grabs your attention. Once you've noted that, allow your awareness to go to the opposite end, and note what you sense there. Sometimes people say, "Nothing," and are very confused. They think they did the exercise incorrectly. However, the truth may be that "nothing" is exactly the quality that is present, a kind of nothingness or space. Maybe it feels empty or invisible. We're just observing here. There is no judgment, no right or wrong answer.

Now that you have noticed the thing that is something and you have noticed a no thing, which is the nothing,[3] then allow both of those qualities to occupy your awareness at the same time and surrender it, let go of it. Notice what happens. Most of the time people will experience the two qualities mingling and morphing as the pressure equalizes, balancing each other out. Just be present and notice what happens.

We're going to continue the same thing with each of the other directions. When moving forward or back, where does your attention go first? Are you more forward? Or are you more back? Just note that.

Once you've noted what there's more of, then note what there is less of. Usually it will be an opposite quality. As you did before, allow these opposites to occupy your awareness at the same time. Then release them and notice what happens.

Next we'll check the horizon, from side to side, and then release it. Sometimes people will feel one side as more dense and the other less present, or one side larger and the other smaller, but whatever it is for you, notice that. When the sides blend and balance, the horizon opens. Again, allow the opposite to be present in simultaneous awareness, and then let go of it all and notice what arises from the release.

Last, we will observe the energy on the inner and the outer. Is your energy more concentrated inwardly, or is it more active outside and around you? Sometimes it can feel like chaos or static or like a shell. Or it may feel like nothing, just vast open space. Or maybe it is the opposite, tight, held in, or stuck. Again notice the opposite qualities of the inner and outer, then let go and receive the balancing effect of the some-thing, the no-thing, and the everything. Simply notice this and that, here and there, the something and nothing, the particle and the wave, the differential upon which quantum physics is based. As long as the viewer attempts to focus on both the particle and the wave at the same time, these two will cancel each other out––and here is where new forms of potentiality reside.

Including It All

So what is happening? Is the charge disappearing? It feels like that, like it just evaporates. But really all we're doing is noticing where the charge is and is not, which is where our awareness is or is not, and then we are getting out of our own way so that these energies can return to their natural balance without our mental, emotional, or physical influence running the show. If we are not conscious of where we are energetically, we may be enacting an unconscious pattern—living the habit. By practicing this simple exercise, we are interrupting old patterns of habit and teaching ourselves flexibility. What we can do in the immediacy of the moment is to relieve the dynamics of pressure of the stuckness and collapse anxiety, tension, or whatever it is by focusing our awareness momentarily this way, loosening the grip of habit, which aids in returning to wholeness again and again.

Isn't it interesting, the word *attention*? A tension. Where you get stuck is where your attention is. That's the first giveaway that you are out of balance. The skill is to learn to focus without tension. To be in open awareness, witnessing all of it at the same time. Once the skill has been developed, you won't need to do this exercise of embodying the simultaneity of focus and openness. Meanwhile, just practice returning to the balance of your inherent wholeness.

So far I've kept this exercise simple. For now, let's keep to this form, allowing it to be this simple. Continue to practice these basic directions of movement, noting their qualities and holding the opposites in your awareness with equality. Then presence all of what you have noticed simultaneously, without preference for one or the other. We have not considered spiritual-psycho-emotional issues yet. However, you may see them hinted at in the following layout. Let us review:

The Energetics of Balance Exercise
Presencing the Four Polarities of Movement

Note each direction. Hold the opposites in
open awareness. Let go and receive.

Up and down = *universe and earth*

Forward and back = *future and past*

Side to side = *feminine and masculine*

In and out = *micro and macro*

When you make the two one, and when you make the inside like the outside, and the outside like the inside, and the above like the below, and when you make the male and the female one and the same, so that the male may not be male nor the female female...then you will enter the Kingdom.

    —Jesus, Gospel of Thomas 22 (Layton), Gnostic Scripture

What we have been experiencing here is a holographic matrix,[4] a simple path to integration. Every distortion is a matrix of untapped potential ready to be birthed and expressed. It is interesting that the word *matrix* is a Latin derivative of *māter,* meaning "mother." It suggests that one form, as a vessel, carries the creation of another. In this exercise, we are blending form and formlessness: the physicality of our body in tandem with the energetic pattern of perception at any given moment—a three-dimensional boundary of light. We are consciously tapping into the container of our soul body while training ego to trust the subtle energetic nature of soul. We are both contained and whole, simultaneously fluid and resilient.

This principle can be applied in an infinite number of ways to all areas of life— thoughts, emotions, and physicality.

This is the power of presencing Something, Nothing, and Everything.

Our being is so finely attuned to equanimity that we can always return to our natural state of balance simply by being true to the moment, by presencing *what is* and *what is not*. We are seeking to meet it all without judgment or story, purely opening to what is present this very moment and being with our enoughness. When we presence what is present, our body-mind will instantaneously self-correct, and we will once again feel the flowing freedom of spirit.

Applying Balance to Life

The next step is a bit more advanced. It shows a way to apply this exercise to an issue with which we may be dealing. Let's say, for example, that I'm experiencing a headache. I have taken aspirin, drunk water to hydrate myself, and been assured that I do not need medical attention. So here I am with uncomfortable pain. I pause to notice where it resides; the pain is in my head. Okay, I have located it. What next? Now I will deepen into the sensation, which means I will need to objectively witness what is here without getting swallowed in the looping of any stories with emotional content. If an emotion arises, I simply notice the texture of it. If crying arises, I feel the fluidity of movement. If it is anger, I sense heat or sharpness, and so forth. In other words, I do not act out the emotion, but remain with the sensation. I feel the emotion yet stay on the straight and narrow edge by acting as a witness.

Now I notice that this contraction in my head feels very tight, like a knot. As I am present here, I notice that the knot feels so dense that the texture seems like a metallic ball——cold, hard, impenetrable. There is no movement. It feels solid and fixed, and my head really hurts. I have perceived "what is."

Now let's look at "what isn't." I allow my attention to continue moving throughout my body as I explore the terrain. I begin to perceive subtly a quality so delicate that I almost miss it. This is a clue. I catch the scent of this elusive subtlety and drop in. To my surprise, I sense a vast openness that is quite different from the metallic hardness I am feeling in my head. This other sensation feels as though the floor has fallen out of my pelvis. It feels like the ground has disappeared and there is nothing; there is a sensation of no support. As I explore the quality of this space, I notice a kind of emptiness. I find it interesting that I am noticing both what is above and below. This is the same principle we have just learned.

I am aware of *what is,* which is the knot––something, the thing. I am aware of *what isn't,* which is the space––nothing, the no-thing.

In the next step, I allow my awareness to perceive and be with both sensations equally without changing anything. I am simply meeting and being with it all, allowing both this and that to be here in my awareness at the same time. And then I let go of any attachment of needing it to be a certain way, not making up any stories, not resisting, not defending, not trying to fix it. I just allow what is here to be what it is. I am holding awareness of the opposite quality in simultaneity and surrendering to that as I open to the arising and receiving of what I do not know. Simply put:

I open to and allow it all to Be Here, in full all-encompassing awareness, and then, I let go to that and allow the Mystery to act upon me.

Now we are entering the field of unity, which is integrity, wholeness.

Integrity requires us to include with love all that we have denied, cut off, or hidden. Willingness to be with it all without judgment is the love of genuine acceptance.

This reflects the message spoken by Jesus:

For where two or three are gathered in my name, there I am with them.

—— Jesus, Matthew 18:20 (NIV)

What is the meaning of "two or three"? The "something and the nothing"... and the "including it all"——in other words, the everything, the witness. And what does the Christ consciousness bring? Love. This is not just an idea of love but also the miraculous living intelligence that genuine love bestows.

So let's try this on. Pause for a moment to scan your body. Notice the areas that feel tight, stuck, or hard. These are the places that do not easily flow. Anywhere you encounter this kind of sensation is a disruption of integrity that interferes with feeling whole. This observation is not a judgment but an invitation to bring awareness to whatever has been cut off, denied, or hidden due to a belief or injury about something you did not know how to resolve. To notice with nonjudgmental open awareness brings to light what previously has seemed impossible. Be tender here and allow plenty of space so that the pure expression can complete itself, coming all the way through and returning to clear, natural wholeness. This felt sense of wholeness feels supportive and substantial, reliable and sustainable. Here one feels the truth of integrity. You will have a sense of being grounded and contained in wholeness. You are so finely attuned to equanimity that you need only be true to the moment, to presence what is, and to meet that. Therefore, to see things as they are, free of judgment, is mighty powerful and brings a sense of peace.

The Law of Opposites

With these simple energetic exercises, you are learning the fundamental power of the law of opposites. In *Physicians of the Heart: A Sufi View of the Ninety-Nine Names of Allah*, Meyer, Hyde, Muqaddam, and Kahn eloquently express Allah's "Opposite Qualities":

> *Mevlana Jalauddin Rumi says the secret of Allah is found between the opposites. Looking deeply into pairs of opposite divine Names is interesting and significant.... At this point in the process, a transcendent divine Name often suggests itself. Such a Name includes in its meaning both the apparent opposites and transcends the opposites.*[5]

The words *Allah* and *God* refer to the *"ineffable reality, the essence of all things."* This basic ground of reality brings with it a sober view of truth, seeing things purely as they are. Truth integrates all the distorted, fragmented views and voices vying for our attention. When we honor the basic truth without twisting and contorting our view and open objectively, a new kind of stability occurs, thus inhabiting the fullness of being.

I believe that I now understand in some small measure why the Buddhist goes on pilgrimage to a mountain. The journey is itself part of the technique by which the god is sought. It is a journey into Being; for as I penetrate more deeply into the mountain's life, I penetrate also into my own. For an hour I am beyond desire. It is not ecstasy, that leap out of the self, that makes man like a god. I am not out of myself, but in myself. I am. To know Being, this is the final grace accorded from the mountain.

—Nan Shepherd, *The Living Mountain*[1]

Chapter 12

Being Present, Stopping and Dropping

T he last chapter shows the strengthener called surrender and the reliability of Presence. As you learned before, presence is pre-essence.
And essence is love, the truest, purest, most refined quality of Authentic
Self, our Soul. So to develop and grow the capacity for constant contact
with our innate wisdom of guidance, we need to be more and more
present in daily life. But how do we do that?

I remember that in 1989, while on a group break and walking the
beach, I noticed

*... gossamer bubbles popping away, sand's moist tongue wrapping
my feet... sinking in, swallowing, toes wiggling...into the soft belly
of earth...*

While on a break at a residential retreat led by Faisal in Hawaii, a
student asked me how many hours a day I meditated. One might

imagine that the wife of a powerful spiritual teacher would meditate a lot——all day perhaps. But to the dismay of this seasoned practitioner, I responded, "I don't meditate in the traditional sense." I shared that in fact, the best I could do even after having been a student of this teaching for many years was simply to stop whatever I was doing in the moment, pause, and check in by sensing what was present whether it be a thought, sensation, or emotion. And that's what I did for a long time until my body could actually tolerate the intensity and revved charge I felt presencing in focused meditation. I called this Stopping and Dropping, Noticing and Sensing. It happened that fast, over and over again, the whole day. Check in, check in, check in. I developed this way of practice for myself because it was excruciating to sit and be present with my body for any length of time without fidgeting, feeling panicked, or entering a stupor.

By then I was well aware that I had historical, repeating patterns, and I wanted to shed light on these. I knew that to access the answers, I would need to learn how to rest into my body because it held the hidden secrets. Practicing only bite-sized portions of being present helped me a lot. The first clue to seeking more answers arose after my osteopath asked me to go home and write down all the car accidents I had been in. I was shocked to realize the number was fourteen! No way; and yes, sadly it was true. I even discovered a pattern to the type of accident as well as what was said after the fact by those who had hit my car. It was the same response over and over——they did not see me. I was invisible. Either the sun was in their eyes or they were looking somewhere else, but most of all, I wasn't there. All those incidents, except for two, happened while I was sitting at a red light. Time and again my braked car was what had stopped them. And many of the drivers were far exceeding the speed limit. Needless to say, I went through a lot of cars, not to mention the toll on my body, psyche, and nervous system.

Once I understood that pattern, I was not hit again. What a relief. And to top it off, while sitting at those long lights, I would often space out, staying unconscious and thus reinforcing not being seen. Yet it wasn't until the mid-1990s that I became fully aware of my brain injuries and effects of PTSD. This occurred while studying the Touch Resolution of Trauma work, an innovative bodywork training developed by Kathy Kain that became the hands-on approach for the Somatic Experiencing (SE) work of Peter Levine. Without consciously knowing it, I had developed for myself, years earlier, a resourcing protocol. And those teeny tiny steps I took along the way had accumulated and grown until I could actually sit with ease in meditation for a substantial length of time pain free and without panicking to get away.

As a child I had an incredible sense of being invisible. Even when dancing on stage, I felt a hollow emptiness and was afraid to be seen. My invisibility cloak was so pervasive that once while at a crowded beach in southern California when I was ten years old I got swept out to sea in an undertow, and no one noticed. As I churned in the force of the waves pinning me down in the sand, a huge suction grabbed and pulled me through an underwater tube-like formation, sucking me far away from the shore. I couldn't breathe and fought to get to the surface. But the more I struggled, the more fierce the turbulence. At last I succumbed to the fact that I might drown, and in that moment of surrender, I was released. I popped to the surface like a cork far away from the shore.

Discovering Unconscious Patterns

Everything that has ever happened to us is stored in body memory. Within every cell is a matrix of our entire history and more. Our connective tissue wears it, our organs wear it, and so on. This body mapping wears an energetic imprint that endures even when the cells die and are replaced. What happened in the past was laid down, eventually becoming a pattern, an unconscious program, an automatic response. Yet consciousness can un-create the relationships we have had if we pause to claim choices not yet dreamed possible.[2]

Our impulses arise from what we *do* or *don't do* over time, coming primarily from unconscious energetic patterns in body memory.[3] Yet if we slow our attention, which brings fuller awareness and stretches time, while presencing the sensation in the body, we can remember. However, being aware is not always comfortable, which is why so many of us do not remain present. Some memories are pleasant, but many are not. And unpleasant memories can elicit an upheaval of overwhelming emotion.

When folks hear about the work I do, they often remark, "I don't do that kind of stuff. As far as I'm concerned, the past is past." But you see, the past is actually present. We are enacting it all the time unconsciously, automatically, through our opinions, reactions, and the way we walk in this world. And the more the personality drives the charge, the wider the resulting chasm because the unconscious pattern doesn't know how to change. The personality will avoid realignment, because avoidance is avoiding the clarity of the void, if you remember. Or it will bolster itself up, defending its position as a distraction from feeling the deficiency.

In sum, there is even a story about our story, which creates a secondary line of defense. First we must become aware of the story we tell about the story. Then we get to meet the story. But if we keep on telling that same story over and over, we are actually avoiding the next step by reinforcing what we already know. Just like the ouroboros, the symbol of the snake swallowing its tail, we must quiet our wagging tongue and dizzying mind and swallow the "tale" of our never-ending story. Then a new cycle, a new beginning can commence. The misunderstanding is to think it is all about the story. It is and it isn't—truly a paradox.

This work is not about digging up the past. Even so, awareness of the past may arise if there is something *our being* is asking us to be present with, which brings us back to presence. Whatever the wound, essence will remedy. And essence is a segue between mind and body. If we find ourselves looping by retelling the story (mental), we cannot access what is in the body (instinct). Here it is helpful to notice if the impulse in the body is turned toward or away from life? How we wear that charge and the meaning we give to it is the underpinning impulse that initiates the force that drives the story. When we pause amid whatever is going on and drop in to here, opening to the observer, our witnessing self, we can draw upon new insight. And that insight will illuminate what we were unable to see, setting us free. Like the snake swallowing its tail, we taste eternal unity.

Perceiving What Is Essential

Essence is thus perceived through the trinity of mind-body-witnessing awareness. We all experience our essence, but the experience is not usually sustainable. Many folks meet their essential self when they are falling in love, or taking a special vacation in a beautiful setting, or doing something extraordinary such as having a wedding, promotion, or baby. In moments of newness, the mind is expansive and open, bodily sensations are pleasurable, and the breath is ease-full. Life is more simple yet free in every way. We experience witnessing, perceiving, and sensing all at the same time. All is present here. These are special moments, loving and rich, but the average person can neither understand nor continuously create such situations. Hence, when we are not in circumstances where *all is well,* it is crucial to enlarge our capacity of objective witnessing.

We have the opportunity at such times to diffuse any charge that would build momentum. Momentum rides on emotion because emotion is motion. The more the charge builds, the more cathartic it becomes, possibly offering some emotional release. However, this ride can eventually sweep us into a trauma vortex, which flames hysteria, fear, shame, blame, grief, or hostility. Before we know it, we could be overwhelmed or acting it out. With too much focus on the body or the emotion, we may lose objectivity. We can get stuck in the loop, isolating and merging with sensation so much that we create even more separation. And the more separation, the scarier it gets. 'Round we go, perpetuating more of what we wish to avoid, believing we are doing the opposite! Mercifully, some therapeutic modalities help to transform these cathartic energies, but they are mainly used during supervised sessions and lessons.

Our process can go to the other extreme as well. Forgetting to sense the body and giving too much ungrounded awareness to spaciousness, we allow that spaciousness to grow and expand. Without a counterbalance, too much space can become a dissociative, spaced-out, no-"body"-home experience. We split off and feel nothing; we brace and go numb. What we are learning here is to grow our skills to be with it all, to be more here. To be present is to open to our True Self, the true nature of our Natural Essence—the subtle body.

Without the witness present, all the stuff of the mind and emotions spill, leaving us to struggle. We are stuck in anger and doubt with whatever we are unable to resolve because the resolution of transformation can be remedied only by the physician of the heart. Here is a poem describing one student's recognition of such a passage. It reveals the wisdom he received as a result.

In Love You Will Be Found

Far away, off in the distance
Is a man at play.
She comes closer now
Nearing the end of day,

Sitting beneath the mighty tree
Head bowed down
Resting on his knees,
She came to him
With a smile wide and bright,
A beauty from the darkness
Her head and shoulders high and upright,
Full of only gifts and
Things made right.

Nowhere to go,
Nothing left to give,
She stands beside him
Losing his will to live.

Lying and fighting
The anger rages out,
A mere mortal man
Alone and dying of doubt.

No match for demons
And gods or shadows of the past,
Thinking so foolishly
He could make the goodness last.

She stands in witness
As the mythic battle unfolds,
Standing as a suffering mother yearns,
"Come back and join the fold."

Wanting only relief
From the pain which knows
No bounds,
Wounded and weary
Reach out
And in love
You will be found.

———Fran DiBiase[4]

Bringing along the objective awareness of our "witness" self while being present with that very feeling we are wishing to avoid brings the precise medicine that is needed. Often our salvation is what we least expected the outcome to be! Here, in a world of opposites, the nourishments of soul beckon our ego to rest in her loving arms.

I have a dear friend and mentor, a delightful cohort in mischief, Alan Gutman, MD. I appreciate his out-of-the-box thinking, such as this brilliant statement, "Rational thinking prevents us from going into the dangerous place that's safe." It means that often what we think is unsafe and dangerous is in reality the very movement that will liberate us!

In 2002 we developed a methodology of presencing called Living!Source, which we co-taught. We played with dual/non-dual relationship. One feature of the session was our version of the Stopping and Dropping exercise. We even thought of making bracelets with the steps written on them to support folks' practice! We came up with a half-dozen renditions. Although I was already practicing my own version of this work, there is no fixed way, no right or wrong. But it is necessary to include all of the ingredients to achieve presencing. So here in current form is yet another way of Stopping and Dropping, living from the *effulgent radiance of being.*

As you become more adept, I invite you to adjust your own practice to a version that is most resonant to you.

Presencing Exercise
Stopping and Dropping

STOP ~ Pause and Orient
Where are you? Are you present or not present, in balance or out of balance? Note that.

DROP ~ Check In
Where is your focus coming from? Is it more mental, emotional, physical, or spaced-out?

NOTICE ~ What's Here
What is the energetic movement of the story, issue, feeling? Charged, stuck, empty?

SENSE ~ Perceptual Awareness
What is the quality of the energy, such as the size, shape, color, texture, or density?

OPEN ~ What Else
What's not that? What is the rest of the environment like, the surrounding space?

WITNESS ~ Include It All
Welcome it all with open awareness——the something, the nothing, and the everything.

LET GO ~ Be in the Flow
Surrender and rest into the morphing of arising intelligences re-organizing what is here.

RECEIVE ~ Feel the Gratitude
Appreciate the generosity of the gift emerging; receive the quality of essence.

Remember that *essence* means love. Whatever the aspect or quality of essence you receive, know that it is a specific kind of love needed to heal or correct what has been out of alignment or creating havoc in your life. If you were in a state of chaos, you may now feel a sense of calmness or peace. This is a loving peace, patient and understanding, connected with the beauty of a deeper, fuller mystery.

Now presence the quality of what is here. Is it silky, smooth, buoyant? What do you sense? Or maybe you felt sadness, and now you have a sense of sweetness or joy. This love brings specific nourishment, a honeyed elixir of the soul. Each of these substances of essence is different, yet both are love. The soul reflects many more qualities of this generative, nutritive Essence. It is the frequency of this light that is your love...whispering to you of your beauty.[5]

Section Four

Reflections

Star of wonder, star of light
Star of beauty, star so bright.
Intrinsic nature of my soul
Starlight may you ever glow.

Star of mystery, inner sight
The Source giver all my life.
Star essential, star that's me
When we are one, I'm so free.

Star light, star of life
Chandelier, body of light
Totality, you are complete
Treasure, my soul to keep.

Vehicle of my soul
The light giver make me whole.
Star of wonder, star of light
Star of beauty, star so bright.

—— Cheri Dale, *A Garden of Songs*, children's CD[1]

Chapter 13

Visitations and
Gifts of Other Realms

My visitations were exposures, informed glimpses, revelations from
the other side in which the veils were lifted. This contact was
easily accessed and for periods lasting a year or several at a time when
the ability to see, hear, and perceive the mystery was profoundly heightened. For the younger me, there was no context in which to hold these
visitations, for my reality was not like others' around me. I realize in
hindsight that each of the openings was preceded by a traumatic event,
a life-changing occurrence, or some other kind of extreme physical or
emotional duress. Like a fault line shifting, the openings would come
only after sudden change. And through that crack, the light shone in. I
could entrust my sightings to very few, and so it was my good fortune
to have a mother who not only accepted and understood but also supported my multisensory tendencies by directing me to resources where I
could further develop my abilities.

Many of the episodes revealed beings of light and other forms of life. These intelligences showed me that reality is not what it seems. As a child I had learned early on not to discuss my experiences. Such sightings were often judged as the stuff of fantasy, the outcome of non-conformity, due to a narcissistic need to be special, or just downright crazy. Yet through the grace of the phenomena working upon me, I knew better than to doubt myself. Each direct experience tuned me to a higher, less audible frequency than what most folks experience. These inoculations of love were impeccably timed to make it possible for a sensitive child to stay in this denser world, where periodic hauntings lingered and sometimes tempted me to leave the body. The consistent presence of the light-beings provided a loving connection to the inner sacred part of myself.[2] A wisdom thread thus ran through all my "lessons" from the other side:

> *We come from love, are made of love, and——no matter what happens to us——we are love. To know this love is to understand that by our very nature we are of the light. To turn away from our light is to forget who we truly are, and to forget who we truly are is the most painful experience we can ever have.*

Love, light, and truth form a synergistic relationship, each enhancing the other. When we view life from love, this love shines light anywhere there is misalignment about truth. Although my teachings left me with profound experiences, I also received the uncomfortable knowing of places where there was incongruence. So any change in my life that arose from this awareness affected everything else at once, which made more and more sense as I matured. Eventually in adulthood, I was able to accept the disturbing distortion that while my mother had been my psychic protector, she was also my jailor by the denial of the truth about my origin. And I say this with great compassion for the suffering that we have all endured.

These realizations collided within me when my son was an infant. I vowed to do everything in my power differently than what I myself had gone through at his age. There are tricky edges when a child is born of our flesh. The biological imprints can be both confusing and compelling. The force of our unconscious patterns is still present, and we automatically act them out unless they are consciously dealt with. For the momentum of the energetic pathways that we ourselves went through, as well as those that our mothers experienced during the different stages of our growth, feel like force fields pushing us along in the same way. It requires tremendous awareness to not automatically enact the past and to shift our programmed trajectory toward making new choices.

I reflected deeply on my journey when my son was eight months old, the same age I was when my birth parents had divorced. My young mother, who was distraught over the condition of her life, attempted suicide. While holding me in her arms, she wept, whispered her love, and expressed how she felt incapable of providing for me. She slipped away, unconscious from an overdose. Merged with her, I floated in a disorienting death-like bardo, not yet realizing the clear luminosity of the brilliance right here.

My mother was taken far away to an institution, and I became the ward of my father. He was a rodeo cowboy who traveled the circuit, as it happened, and so I came into my grandmother's care. But that was no place for an infant because she had a ranch to run, and so to my auntie's I went. But the stress of caring for me as well as for her own two young ones, plus suffering a husband with no tolerance for my crying, spelled the tipping point of her well-being. Off to the hospital she was taken, and I was passed along to a family friend, mother of three little boys. It was after some time that she and her husband decided they would adopt me. But when I was nearly two, out of the blue my mother reappeared and stole me away. Today they would call it kidnapping, for she left no trace of where we had gone. I later discovered that my dad and his family searched for me ever after.

From that tiny northwestern ranching town, with a population of about 300, I was driven down to the city of San Francisco and into a world I didn't know. When we stepped through the door of her flat, a man stood there. I was told that he was my daddy, but I knew my dad, and it was not so. My mother insisted that my memories were mistaken, and methodologically over the years, I was forced to hide, bury, erase, and deny all the early connections I had known.

When I turned 21, my stepdad revealed the truth that he was not in fact my biological father. It was a tremendous liberation to hear those words. My eyes began to clear from the chronic fuzzy focus I had been living with since I was two. I no longer needed to split off from my reality and the deeply buried memories. Denying the truth had required every ounce of control I could muster to torsion down any hint of my past, which left me subsisting in a chronic state of static.

Later I came to understand that my mother was concerned that my younger half-sisters and I be raised equally. But most of all she worried that if I were to grow up knowing my real dad, I could be lured away by the horses and wild beauty of my homeland, tempted to never return. So, for 16 years I grew up with a hidden identity. Once the full truth was spoken, however, I immediately began searching for my birth dad. It took me three years to find him and ten years to piece together my childhood.

Our bodies remember everything, but the truth can be so deeply hidden that it seems to be forgotten. What I forgot in this case was really denial, which is paralytically erosive.[3] As a result I suffered a kind of low-grade constant depression. I couldn't sustain feelings of joy. So to feel vitality meant that I pushed myself to extremes in order to feel alive. I share my story not to condemn, but simply to shed light on the mechanism of denial, repression, and the devastating effect it can have on mind and body. To cut off our feelings, emotions, and memories creates intense interference and extreme pain. Pain is nothing more that the blockage of energy, and blockages create interference. Interference is the laying down of patterns that obstruct freedom. And until consciousness meets the patterns, we will continue revolving on the hamster wheel, unable to actualize our authentic Self.

As time passed, the discomfort of being in my body loosened in direct proportion to my uncovering of truth. I was now able to change my old self-deprecating devaluing habits and really grow. The patterns don't leave us, but how we relate to them becomes the difference between night and day. We could actually recreate the interference in an instant if we were to go unconscious again. That's why masters continue practicing their practice. This is how we evolve our consciousness and remain free. We are cultivating our capacity to be present so that the less developed aspects of the mind can grow.

I eventually found my birth dad and my surrogate mothers and was able to validate my early memories. I got to know him more before he passed on prior to the birth of my son. As painful as was my early childhood, I did get to grow up with a stepfather who provided support and genuinely loved me. Bob was truly the rock of constancy in my life. My parents did the best that they knew. Besides, the 1950s were the days when society held the misconception that young children were unconscious and wouldn't remember their early life. With the advent of neuroscience and somatic teachings, however, this misconception is no longer accepted. In fact, there are many studies to support the intelligence of the unborn and very young child.

The bigger truth is that I wasn't the only one who suffered loss. Every family member and relative who had kept the secret also was affected, as well as my two younger sisters, who always asked why I was the only one with blonde hair and blue eyes. As children, my sisters and I perceived something was amiss——all of us suffered. For to turn away from the truth blackens the heart and places a tremendous strain on the entire organism.[4] On her deathbed, my mother asked forgiveness for what had motivated her to deny the truth——jealousy and fear that I would love my dad more than her. She had carried a stone in her heart my entire life because my existence continuously reflected to her a painful family lie. It was the tragic loss of a brilliant and beautiful being. Before she passed away, we came to terms with that and shared the greatest love that we could know. We were both freed at last.

This was a family constellation pattern that was shared by my mother, my step dad, and my birth father's lineage. My story was their story, and their story was their mother's story and the grandmother's story. It was a tale about the powerlessness they all felt from fathers lost by death or addiction and children taken away or given up for adoption——all perpetuated by fear and inadequacy. Blessed be.

A New Beginning

I am holding my infant son in reverence and gratitude for this beautiful being in my arms, invoking a prayer that I be guided to music that would support and nurture his soul. I am not seeking frivolous kid tunes, but songs of purpose. I pray that he will grow in relationship with the beauty of the world, as well as his inner beauty, to help him to remember who he truly is.

He is nursing now, and all is quiet when in the distance, I hear a faint and gentle voice, a beatific voice, ringing pure and clear. I am resting with my little one, believing the song is wafting through the open window from our neighbors' house. Yet surprisingly, it is drawing closer, dialing in more and more clearly. Curious, I get up and go to the window, leaning into the sound to listen out. But I detect no music coming from out there. I hear only the birds chirping, so I imagine the neighbors have turned it off. I sit back down, continuing to feed and rock my son. No sooner than done, I hear the song again. Perplexed, I get up to see if the sound is coming from the TV downstairs. Yet when I look down, neither is Faisal home nor the TV on. All is silent from below. Confused, I go back to sit with our son.

Little by little, the voice draws nearer. I now realize what is happening! A channel has opened, and I am the conduit. I try listening in earnest, but as soon as I do, everything stops. Catching myself in the act, I pause, let go of trying, and begin resting-in again. The song resumes. The more I let go, the more it effortlessly grows until, word for word and note for note, the angelic voice builds into a choir of seraphim filling the air. An entire song comes through. Excitedly, I reach for my son's toy tape recorder (a gift from Grandpa Bob and Grandma Sharon) and repeat into it the joyful lyrics and melody.

Days and weeks and months passed by. Within a year and a half, forty-seven songs had come through, fulfilling my wish. But instead of buying music for my son, I had been directly gifted his special songs. I was then guided to create a CD that would not only help to grow his connection with being but, as it turned out, was a gift to me, too. I was tenderly reconnected with the preciousness of my own inner child, the magical child within. When the energy had integrated, I opened up even more to unconditional love.[5]

Serendipitously, every step of the way was effortlessly laid out before me. I, who had no prior knowledge of music other than dancing to it, was able to actualize the recording of seventeen of these songs. This journey began with the chance meeting of the gifted musician and singer Helene Attia, who could play by ear. I sang to her every melody, along with the lyrics. She in turn sang and played them back to me on her guitar. We realized then that the songs were special, although they didn't fit in with the commercial market at the time. Nonetheless, we decided to go ahead with the recording project. We both recognized the value of such a gracious gift given by the angels and the benevolence of Source. Because of our fateful and unique meeting, we also knew this was something we needed to do. It was truly a *"Gift"* ~ and this in turn became the most powerful song on the album.

Helene brought in Jack Gates, who contributed his fine talent and incredible collection of rare guitars. And I invited Kit Walker to let loose his muse on the baby grand and synthesizers. Kit had produced and played on Devi Premal's and Miten's first CDs. I was blown away by the mastery of the arrangements these profound musicians offered. We all were held in a miraculous field of blessings and grace, each recording uplifting the next, moving from lively nursery tunes to a rich inner tapestry of intrinsic transmissions from the divine. David Owens recorded and mixed our CD, appreciating the purity and innocence of the music. He treated it with the gentle care one would give a newborn. Then there was Owen Davis, who shined his bright light with body clapping and drums, highlighted by the voices of our children and their friends.

Nine months later, the CD *A Garden of Songs* by Cheri Dale was born. I used my middle name, Cheri, and my birth dad's name, Dale. This event brought full circle the fact that when the songs began, my son was the same age I was when I had lost my mom. And when the CD was done, my son was the same age I was when my mom had showed up again and took me away from my birth dad. It was uncanny how exacting the dates were, although I did not recognize this at the time. I was simply swept by the guidance of Grace and completely surrendered to the unfolding synchronicity that was taking place.

Guided by clairaudience, the songs were a celestially channeled experience, a generous transmission from an angelic choir of unseen beings. And after this completion, my mother passed on. The birth of the album and death of my mom unleashed an undulating wave of receiving and releasing all along. The last portion of the recordings touched upon the delicacy of arriving home. In my mother's final moments, when Helene and I thought the CD was done, this final poignant melody came for my mom...

Dear Mili, are you captured in birdsong, or floating like a flower on a brook?
Dear Mili, are you dancing on wind song, everywhere for you I look?
Guardian angel walks with you; the old man housed you in the wood.
Your star came to earth and guided you; the story of your life is in my book.
Mili, oh, oh, o Mili ~ Mili, I'm looking for you.
Mili, oh, oh, o Mili ~ Mili, I am calling to you.

Decades later, I discovered that the name *Mili* in India means "to meet" or "to find." My mother, the lifelong *seeker* had at last found her *star* of the divine. And the story of her life is indeed in the book of my own DNA, to be loved, cultivated, and actualized. With the advent of my freedom, she too was set free. The circle of connections was now complete.

I find it interesting that as a child, I had a glimpse of one of these songs. I had heard it sung by an angelic voice hovering above me when I was 11 years old. The words were about an Auntie Rosie. I found out years later, when I reunited with my birth dad, that his mother, my Grandma Donna, had had a sister Rosie who adored me when I was a baby. This preverbal history had been stored away in my body-mind memory and the only song that showed up from another time. Yet as that 11 year old, I instinctively knew that its message was part of something much larger. To what and where it belonged, I didn't yet know. I find it fascinating now to look back over my lifetime and see a precise pathway that was laid out all along the way. To the wisdom of this Guidance, I humbly bow.

Just tune into nature until you feel the love flow. That is your arrow into the deva world. It does not matter if there is a message or not, it is the state that counts. Always it is your state that the nature world responds to, not what you say, not what you do, but what you are.

—— The Devas, channel to the Findhorn Community[1]

Chapter 14

Phenomena and Entrainment

O ther worldly phenomena bring unexplained occurrences in our physical world. For some time, my watches were unreliable and would randomly stop. I went through untold quantities of batteries and eventually gave up wearing them. I have a lovely collection if you are in need of a watch! Following that phase, I went through a period in which five car engines blew up. No kidding! The first engine died as I was leaving my first marriage and the life I had known. My car was packed to the gills. As I backed out of the carport to drive away, I heard a terrible grinding noise like metal chewing metal. The car had to be towed to a repair shop, where I transferred all my belongings into a rental car. I got back on the road both terrified of change and determined to change. In transit to my new home and while climbing a hill, engine number two blew. How crazy is that? I called the rental place from across the bay. They had to send a tow truck all that way and refused to rent to me again. I wrote that one off as poor maintenance on their part and found another car rental place.

But lo and behold, two weeks later one wintery dark night while crossing the narrow Richmond-Marin Bridge in the wee hours of the morning, the third engine blew, leaving me stranded mid-span and unable to pull over. I had to leave the car and push through the howling wind with ominous, eerie black waves rocking below to reach a call box. That did it! A few days later I went straight to the car dealership and bought a brand new vehicle right off the lot.

I drove for a while without incident, and then. . .boom, my spanking new car blew up its engine, too. Because I had traveled fewer than 1,000 miles, the dealership made repairs without question. Back on the road for only a few months, the same engine blew again. This time I was in a crime-ridden area of San Francisco at midnight, the last car in the parking lot to leave the set after shooting a commercial in the warehouse district. My confidence was severely shaken by now. Receiving such echoes from my early childhood, five homes and now five engines, I felt jinxed. I did deep inner work about my fear of existence. With all the setbacks, it took great effort to work and function in the world, but I was determined to get to the root of this pattern.[2]

Concerning the cars, it was determined that all five engines shared one thing in common—–the engine bearings had failed in each case. What are the odds of that? If you understand how engine bearings work, you will note the exact parallel regarding previous traumatic themes in my life, such as being born prematurely as a result of a catapulting accident and collapsing while dancing amid the driving pressures of colliding events. Just as the momentum of activities gone overboard can cause disarray in life, worn or misaligned bearings can tamper with the forces created by the rods and pistons and dislodge the crank shaft. The pattern of interference in the regulation of reciprocating movement versus balanced rotation (whether in a body or an engine) was at work in both instances. It couldn't have been more precise.

In the dealership where I had bought the new car, my case was met with keen interest. Certain there would be some fault with my driving ability, they tested my skills and found them satisfactory. Clearly, I wasn't the cause. Intrigued, they really wanted to figure this out. So I opened up and shared the fact that five engines were left with ground up bearings in the past year and a half. Then I leaned in and asked, "Do you suppose a person could be behind all of this?" I told them about my divorce, that my ex was an engine builder specializing in high performance racing engines, and that he had been stalking me.

They took all this information to a team of experts at national headquarters and responded with, "It's unexplainable." Because the hood was locked from the inside and the bearings were deeply internal, no one could have tampered with the engine. "We have no explanation why this has happened so many times. On our end, we will call it a lemon with a computer error, but that's a long shot." Again they repaired it. By now I had had enough, and so I sold the car below value to someone I knew, giving them all the sordid details of its history. I saw the car periodically over the years, and it never had that problem again.

While all of this was going on with car engines, I also had to move five times within that same year and a half! Homes were disappeared out from under me due to all manner of unexpected situations on the part of the landlords, from nervous breakdowns, to homes being sold suddenly and in-laws needing the space, and so on. I ended up living in a 9- by 13-foot cottage with all my belongings. Reminiscent of the pea under the princess' mattress, my belongings were stored under my bed, which had been lifted five feet off the ground! Midway I was sure I would have a breakdown with so much uncontrolled craziness going on. The level of free-floating fear I experienced was outrageous. My life was a lemon! Yet it turned around and instead became a most empowering period for me. I experienced a pivotal change, an awakening, as I left behind monumental false structures and limiting beliefs. Stepping head on into the unknown, I felt my overt fear and repressed anger collapsing in the face of new challenges, transmuting into a higher form of consciousness.[3] I courageously claimed my existence, my life! With that came immense gratitude and self-love.

Embracing the Mystery

The year was 1985, and without hesitation I fully embraced the mystery of the next phase of my life. This period lasted ten years and brought with it punctuations of energy shifts highlighted by periodic phenomena, such as fans turning on and off spontaneously when I walked into a room. These incidents came in groupings in various locations just in case I might decide to write them off as coincidental. Over time, I discovered that the more subtle and refined my perception, the more the world as I knew it would turn upside down. My delicate and refined sensitivities opened up new gateways of awareness to profound, rarely spoken-of realities. I could no longer hide my mystical tendencies. For me, some periods were so disorienting that I dared not mention them because they seemed at odds with basic beliefs grounded in rationality. These topics at the margins were often met with hostility. I had seen it before in others who either got locked up or medicated when the unexplainable showed up. But by now, I had the skills and experience to understand what was really going on. These were private, personal, internal, enlightening experiences, and I had no need to defend or prove their existence.

Then in 1996, I met a holy man, a shaman who told me not to let myself be disturbed by any incongruities, for I was remembering and experiencing gifts of merit. He said I had gained these gifts from lifetimes of preparation. He counseled me that not many could understand my capacity, but that one day, when the time was right, I would share my story. It has taken nearly 20 years to process and articulate this passage––to be clear of interfering blocks and bow to the brilliant guidance of Wisdom. It is not for me to get in the way of what is asking to come through, ready to be shared and taught to others. But more than that, it has been for me, as I hope it will be for you, a way to exemplify what is innately true. I have touched the living Source we truly are and begun to clearly differentiate between the territory of ego and the terrain of essence.

It is important that I share the phenomenological occurrences of this time not because of the events themselves but for what shifts in myself were necessary to sustain contact. It was a conundrum that the more balanced and integrated I became, the more refined and sensitive my perception. My extra-ordinary life did not jive with the day-to-day reality of the majority of individuals in our society. Not only did it fry my circuits, I was left unfit for the herd consensus. To the lower brain, my new life triggered danger, because our primitive wiring expects being like the tribe to assure safety and survival. It is always a courageous step to depart from the status quo. After decades of integrating all manner of contrasting energies, I can now demonstrate that it is indeed possible to function in a linear time-based society and still maintain circular-time sensitivity as a nondual being in the world's dual reality.

And yes, just in case you wonder, to this day the jets in my bathtub randomly turn themselves on; or I may hear a music box, an angelic chorus, or a bell chiming in the ethers; or I may feel emotional impressions and receive inner sight when touching objects. Eventually, I came to terms with the simple fact that it requires more effort to block awareness than to surrender to the coexistence of the supernatural reality in which we are all living. And I learned to be at peace with the fundamental fact that we have been conditioned backward to believe that natural phenomena are unnatural, when what is really unnatural is to block what is natural! May you also be able to open to and embrace the fuller you![4]

Stepping Back With Wonder

Stepping back, let's pause for a second to consider some of the repeating patterns in your life. What message from your unconscious is asking to be awakened? Like in the fairy tale of *Sleeping Beauty*, what magic kiss will open the kingdom, what hidden message is waiting to be decoded? Take the scenario of my five car engines blowing up. I could have stayed stuck in the fear, feeling like a victim, yet I believed on some level that there was a hidden message to be discovered.

When I allowed myself to have a more spacious look, I was able to see what would not have been possible from a more limited view. I was able to see a truth that was bigger than I had been aware of. I felt it popping the illusion, offering me a brand-new start. I allowed it to re-orient me to life in a way I had not known before. How did that happen?

It happened because I was willing to ask the question, *"If a car is a vehicle, what does the vehicle symbolize?"* My body. *"What part of the vehicle keeps breaking down?"* The engine. *"So if my body is the vehicle, what part would cause me to stop in my tracks if it malfunctioned?"*

There could be a lot of answers here, but primarily, if the brain stops, the body can still go on living. But if the heart stops, everything in the body would cease. So for me, the engine represented my heart. *"And what does the heart represent?"* Love. *"Does someone else's love run my vehicle, or is self-love needed to keep the engine running? Which one is sustainable."* Self-love. It places a great burden on others to attempt to fill our lack of love for self. And it causes great angst for us to desperately grasp outside of our own self to gratify this deficiency...

Gifting Love

It is late at night, the baby is asleep, and Faisal is away teaching in another state. I am flooded with inspiration and quietly drawing by candlelight when I become acutely aware of a watching presence. Electricity fills the air and hairs are standing on end all over my body. Cautiously, my gaze turns toward my bare forearms, confirming that the hairs are truly standing straight out! The presence has come in from behind, and I now feel that it is somehow next to me. Squinting my eyes, terrified at what I might see, I slowly turn. Gingerly, I glance over my shoulder where I view something bobbing or standing––that is, standing, but not, with a buoyant form that does not fit into any rational reality of a being...yet here it is, only it's a dimension of pulsating points of light, brilliant silvery violet-blue neon lights suspended in a holographic space. I detect sparkling particles of light-like stars, an entire universe in the shape of a child-like three-foot body.

Going past panic at the initial shock, I carefully turn my whole self to face this being. I call it a "being" as I sense the palpable presence, intelligence, and aliveness that is near. I am unsure of what might happen and feel a soft sonar wave wash through me. An emanating, loving radiance, immensely pure and clear, communicates to me...telepathically...that it has been with me a long time, and now I am ready to see. There is such love. I carefully and slowly ease myself to stand, legs shaking, feeling cautiously more comfortable now. I take a few steps to see what will happen. To my sheer delight, and with undulations of inexpressible excitement in every cell, my own being is swelling with love as we move in slow motion through the room. I am giddy with laughter alongside my Casper companion. We move up the stairs, and slowly the multidimensional being dissolves, fading from view. I am grateful for this visitor from another realm, preparing me and us for the next phase of our evolution.

This experience, along with others, has helped me to develop deep compassion––for everyone, including myself. I have lost some of my closest relationships because people often fear what they themselves have not experienced or understood. To avoid feeling discomfort, their most common reaction is denial. They may react to others' reality as a bunch of malarkey or as delusional and crazy. Because I love these folks and accept them as they are, it is easy to forgive what they do not know. But equally important is to not doubt or deny what my own experience has been.

Forgiving Our Limitations

How poignant were the words of Jesus when he had to endure hatred and punishment on the cross. He said, "Forgive them, Father, for they know not what they are doing." Until one has had to deal personally with persecution from a trusted friend or acquaintance, he or she cannot really understand the full meaning of these words. The person with an unusual experience can appear schizophrenic, yet such events are not necessarily the result of a split-off fantasy. They are more likely the result of transitions and guiding forces that bring awakening and a fuller scope of understanding a barely perceivable, palpable reality. My wish for those who have had such encounters is that my story may help confirm yours.

The most profound lessons during the visitations were on occasions when I was caught in the mindset that what I was encountering was harmful. It was not until I became calm that I could perceive my situation as quite the contrary. In fact, the terror I was feeling already lay inside of me; it was mine. It was not because of anything others were doing, which was just reflecting the perfect frequency of love. The presence of their energy simply amplified the limitation of where I was not! That was painful. These visitations brought opportunities for stretching my capacity to include other points of view. I was called to bequeath forgiveness and compassion in every direction, much like morning dew spreads upon the petals of a rose mirroring the all-pervading continuum of unconditional love.[5]

As a teacher, I cannot determine a student's experience. That depends on his or her soul path. What I can do is help others to see, sense, and understand their blockages in relation to their soul essence. I can also help them to detect those subtleties and nuances easily passed by, overlooked, or not recognized as valuable. These are sometimes most subtle yet so worthy that they are the very key to the most precious aspects of who a person truly is. These markers can help to free one's ability to claim, embody, and live from that knowledge. That I can help with. My greatest joy in being alive is to help people reconnect with Source, to share what is true and live from that!

"On the mirror of shapes

there's no motion, not a bit;

Because something not

glorious cannot appear on it."

—— Makutbat Imam Rabbini[1]

Chapter 15

Intuition and Body Mapping

To this point, I have primarily spoken about the mind-body-soul relationship from an esoteric, energetic, and egoistic perspective, demonstrating through personal example how intuition is a thread that connects all areas of life whether we are aware of it or not. I have given exercises that have helped me as well as countless students to hone perceptual skills that teach how to become our own biofeedback transformer. Now let's look at scientific research that supports the process of intuition.

The field of neuroscience has grown rapidly during the last few decades. In their brilliant book *The Body Has a Mind of Its Own*, science writers Sandra and Matthew Blakeslee offer complex, cutting-edge research about the brain written in easy-to-understand language. I will simplify the information about these recent revolutionary studies even more, highlighting a few discoveries that relate specifically to what I have been sharing.

Mirroring and Mapping

What we now know about mental, emotional, and physical health and well-being is that the more we use our brain, the more it grows. Not only are good nutrition, focused meditation, and cognitive exercise support for the brain but also using and moving the whole body are necessary activities for brain growth. The *British Journal of Sports Medicine* published a study in 2013 showing that aerobic exercise actually produces brain growth, meaning that we can grow more gray matter, the circuit board for the entire mind–body connection. Now, get ready to expand your view!

The moment you look at others, you instantly download in your own body the entire map of their body. That's right, your body also receives a direct reading of their thoughts, emotions, and sensations. The science behind this instantaneous impression is found in what are called mirror neurons. The mystic yogis have known about, practiced, and taught this for eons, and I learned about this ability in a Mind Dynamics course I took in 1970! Currently, this information is not only being shared openly but also has been proven scientifically. We are living in exciting times when technologies are assisting scientists to understand how brain neurons comprise the elements of certain body maps and detect motion in the premotor cortex of our brain—the insula, cingulate, and secondary touch cortex. This area has to do with how we learn and connect by what we see, through mimicking, and in perceiving empathy, hidden persuasion, sensation, and sexuality. We are learning through watching.[2]

Mirror neurons represent both the witnessing and the experiencing of certain feelings and emotions. You can both feel others' pain and feel their pleasure. When you see their suffering, you feel their suffering as well; when you see their joy, you feel their joy. You perceive by looking and learn by watching, which is one reason why the YouTube channel has been such a success. It is also why I recommend that students attend follow-up and drop-in classes, where they can witness and learn through each other's experience.

Mirror neurons also make it possible for an injured athlete to view her sport from the sideline while in remission, stepping back into the game without missing a beat. Likewise, online pornography has reached epidemic proportions because viewers can feel the sensations of pleasure without having to encounter performance anxiety or risk the emotional intimacy required of a real-life relationship. Research also shows that in autism, the number of mirror neurons is unusually low. Autistic individuals are missing the necessary neurons to connect with the feelings and expressions of others. Nor do they learn by seeing and doing, which is how most education has been set up. In an article in *Science Daily*, however, research by Dr. Ramachandran shows that such individuals can learn by watching themselves. In other words, their mirror neurons respond to their own motion. The study goes on to say that autistic learners need slower movement, slower instruction, and more time to process. By watching themselves move in front of a mirror, and by listening to or sensing themselves through biofeedback, they can grow vital neurons, becoming normal by adulthood.

We are born with a certain number of these specific neurons at birth, and throughout the years, we grow more. Yet if we actively exercise and develop our presencing capacities, we can increase these neurons to an even greater degree. It has been found that people with great empathy actually have more gray matter in their right frontal insulas.

Instantly Intuiting Others

This brings us to von Economo neurons (NEFs), also known as intuition cells. This special class of cells is found only in humans, great apes, elephants, and whales. Discovered in 1925, these are larger, faster, and more highly connected neurons, allowing us to access "instant knowing." Although found throughout the brain, they are mostly concentrated in the right frontal insula. They map your visceral sensations, social emotions, and moral intuitions. *This is where the mind and body unite* to link with the amygdala and its propensity to monitor strong emotions related to experiences, people, places, and things. The amygdala is also connected to food because this area of the brain maps visceral sensations, including your gustatory experience. This spot is also active when you experience both physical pain and psychic pain, such as in shame, rejection, or having been treated unfairly.

According to scientific data, the job of intuition cells is exactly what we think of when we hear the word *intuition*. As if coming out of thin air, they allow flash-fast insights of knowing and understanding, along with a keen sense of trust or mistrust. This leaves room for us to have a wide range of interpretations that are influenced by personal associations, whether or not we trust our intuition or want to know what is really here.

Now let's include what is called peripersonal space in our body mapping system along with mirror neurons and intuition cells. Peripersonal space is that bubble of space an arm's length around you, which is built right into your brain's mapping system. Thus, we have a real awareness of the field around us as well as that around another person's body. Some cultures are so aware of this field that they consciously overlap their own with others' personal space to feel more connected. However, many cultures allow plenty of personal space so as to not get in each other's way. Our brain includes this space as part of our body. So when it feels like someone is too close or not close enough for comfort, we adjust accordingly.

Our peripersonal space is constantly interacting with whatever comes into its range. This field is what an athlete feels when he is in the zone. He so completely fills the space that he may feel bigger than his actual body, or as if there is more of himself outside the body, or that there is a force bigger than himself that is helping to change shape and form. The question has been long asked whether this is our aura. If you intuit this question, what do you sense?

Considering Autism

Back to the subject of autism, I find it truly amazing that so many children are coming into our world having been diagnosed as autistic. This growing sector of society is wired for a learning style that does not respond well to the old structure still being taught in schools. The old style was suited for the masses, but the new style is asking for individual attention. It is interesting that the ailment most noted in modern society is isolation. Industrialized western civilization suffers from the alienation of human beings tucked away in their own boxes, inside their own rooms with their own screens. Is our population now demanding more one-on-one connection to remedy this situation?

We can argue about all the reasons why autism has increased, but we need to meet what is present. And what we have are individuals not wired to learn through mimicking others but set up from birth to mirror back themselves. Increasingly, we are learning through a feedback loop of self-watching, creating a biofeedback system of connecting to our own movements.[3] We are teaching ourselves in a mirror, mentoring ourselves through one-on-one guidance. If we consider this situation as a positive, perhaps we are building a new society of artists at a time when the arts are being cut from funding. Who knows?

For the new world, we will need to learn self-reflection. We will need capable guides to walk their talk in this way. I would be quite happy if we had more of such one-on-one practices, providing edgy learning arenas in a future that is opening to the novel and the unknown.

We have been shown both sides of the coin: how we see and interpret ourselves through the movements of others, and how we see using our own reflection to look back at us. To gaze into the larger view of this mirror is to see ourselves in the outer world extending as far as we can see. And to gaze upon our image mirrored back invites an inner world of reflection. Yet if we bring these two perspectives together in mutual cooperation, we have a reality bigger than either one alone. Ours is a fractal uni-verse going on forever with *me*s and *we*s infinitely connected in a grand continuum on both the outer and the inner.[4] *And in the stillness that lies between ~ in this pause ~ our light is seen.*

Heaven and Earth

GIVE ME LIGHT

Ya Allah,
Give me light in my heart and light in my speech,
And light in my hearing and light in my sight,
And light in my feeling and light in my body,
And light before me and light behind me.
Give me, I pray Thee,
Light on my right hand and light on my left hand,
And light above me and light below me.
Oh Lord, increase light within me,
And give me light and illuminate me.

––The Prophet Muhammed, version by
Hazrat Pir Moineddin Jablonsky[1]

Chapter 16

Bringing It Together and Transformation

When you open yourself up to the grace of illumination through self-reflection, transformation and self-realization can naturally occur. Such is the case when refined presence coupled with open awareness act as a buoy afloat an infinite horizon of ocean. Together they bridge sky and sea, allowing for a vast peripheral space to witness more fully the momentum that drives your day-to-day life. This opening prompts a review of what is mirrored back by exposing energetic nuances behind the weighed choices you do or do not make. What you see and how you experience the image that is shown will vary every time. As in tracking any terrain, the topography may present a theme, but rest assured that the exact landscape would eventually change, depending on the most prominent qualities of your environment. If your issue has had to deal with a feeling of deep-seated vulnerability, you might consider letting go of the ego's limited structure to allow a sense of water or vacuous space to arise. Even so, the rigidity of a structure may present you with an inhospitable rocky landscape. Issues of disempowerment and betrayal may trigger an energetic intensity equivalent to embodying the dynamic force of a volcano! And if you have needed to constantly protect yourself from a barrage of verbal or physical attacks, you may have created a defense that feels more like a metal shield when presenced.

Contemplation and reflection can reveal all manner of images and sensations, each leaving a trail of breadcrumbs leading us back home to the realization of whatever we have been compensating, thus inviting our return to the loving and ready embrace of our soul.

In the following whimsical poem, a student exposes her lifelong obsession for perfection. At first, her thought of letting go of the wound-up perfectionism felt scary. Yet over time, as she presenced her way through, an astonishing inner experience arose, offering her feelings of relief and peace with the resulting emptiness of spaciousness. By letting go of her insatiable need to control, she got to experience positive change and to transform the entangled relationship she once had with control.

Lists,
Lists,
Lists upon lists…
Even a list about how to make
The perfect list,
The un-doing of my lists.
One day, they created a storm,
A flurry of wind swept in from the north,
Lifting my lists into the air.
A big black, shimmering crow shot out from nowhere [and]
In one diving swoop, twisting and turning,
Caught all of my lists, every one!
They dangled down from both sides of his beak.

Flapping in the wind, they taunted me.
I watched them all fly away.
The strangest thing then happened.
The crow, while still in my view,
Burst into flames...
Poof, it was gone.
My lists,
They Done Him In.

—— Juliet Lane[2]

Obsessive control is one way that you may avoid space. Another way is to reinforce the repeating patterns of your history through the retelling of your story to yourself and others. But at some point, the ego awakens from the trance of projections and recapitulations to realize that while the original version had some truth, the bigger truth is that whatever happened then is not exactly what is happening right now——other than a new cast of characters who keep the roles filled so you don't feel the loss or feel at a loss of what to do differently.

Recognizing the brilliant precision with which the projections of the past visit again and again, and receiving the invitation to explore with spaciousness what is mirrored back while remaining in our own skin, requires us to include whatever that quality of space is that we are trying to avoid or fill. At this stage, we have to surrender to the nothingness, the emptiness of no "thing," in order to progress. We do this by

* Catching the storytelling as it builds momentum
* Interrupting our grasping and stopping it
* Dropping into the pause letting go of the story
* Opening to the field of inner spaciousness

* Landing in presence here and now
* Trusting the enoughness of that

This very moment of insight, however, can leave us feeling exposed, transparent. The shield of our story has been a defense against naked emptiness, and now the defense is gone. And here we sit without familiar armor.

Our freedom occurs when we no longer make up stories about the meanings of things and let go to the breathing luminosity of our pure nature. In this living movement of creation is the invitation to hold onto nothing and arrive here. And here is home.

To catch oneself in the act of alienating and abandoning the Self requires turning back from where we have come to claim the wholeness of a birthright innately ours. To accept this invitation is to receive and celebrate the awakened vision of Source, opening to potentialities of possibilities through new ways of being.

The Returning to Balance polarity exercise (*Presencing the Four Directions of Energic Opposites,* chapter 11) demonstrates how to self-correct quickly by interrupting the autopilot repetition of your story and move through life more efficiently and wisely. Otherwise, you can get stuck in rumination, distraction, and defense...or just disappear in clever ways. In reality, balance is not a fixed point but an interaction of resiliency through a continuum of engaged movement and pauses. You notice and reorganize again and again...go away from and return again and again...rise and fall again and again...expand and contract again and again...and so on. By noticing where you are and where you are not, you master both integration and flexibility. This practice helps you positively grow a holistic relationship with your own body, heart, and psyche.

Being Willing to Feel Vulnerable

In the 1990s, I made an accidental discovery at an ortho-bionomy residential event (taught by Bettina Seidle and Danaan Lahey) while Danaan was demonstrating a bodywork movement to realign the pelvis based on the principles he called pitch, yaw, and roll. In a moment of insight, I caught myself feeling inadequate about not being able to retain so much new information. Feeling myself spiral into a sense of deficiency, I dropped-in, acknowledging the signs of vulnerability and the sensation of emptiness resulting from not knowing. In that instant, what I was watching being demonstrated and what I was sensing converged. My inner and outer experience shifted and connected in a profound way.

As a result, I embodied an ancient Hermetic concept I had long pondered—*as above so below, as within so without.* I felt the totality of my body and Being, the whole ignited by a simple physical demonstration along with my willingness to feel vulnerability. Hermes' words now made total sense, no longer a mere idea but a self-realized experience of my whole self. Once more I had received confirmation of the holographic unity of our existence landing in my body, perfectly initiated by Danaan's own clear demonstration in tandem with my willingness to let go of any attachment to getting it right!

This practice of dropping in and being willing is so simple. No one talks about it, and yet everyone knows it because the principle is implicit in so many teachings. From my experience, I began to see countless connections and to have multidimensional understanding. The dots linked faster than I could comprehend, illuminating the *diamond body*, the wisdom of my soul. The effects have been profound and far-reaching, unifying any edge of duality.

As my awareness proliferated exponentially, I witnessed the expose' of every chasm within. What a paradox to land in space—as embodied space. But it helped me to understand the felt sense of being grounded in groundlessness. Thus is the cultivation of the resilient container of *the pearl*, the preciousness of being. I now could orient with myself and others in everyday life, sensing myself as a contained drop in the ocean of existence. From this point on, the pendulating force of my spaced-out tendency, coupled with the wound-up tension of hypervigilance, diffused bit by bit, and over time I grew the capacity to be more present.

Traveling Precarious Pathways

Not knowing where we are energetically is a precarious path. At one end of the spectrum, we merge with everyone and everything, leading us to overwhelm and reaction. By amplifying the *no boundary place,* this state often results in drama, hysteria, and chaos. On the other end of the spectrum, we try to control the feeling of being swallowed by the merger, responding with anger, pushing back, or withdrawing our energy. In that moment, we need to recognize what we are doing. Right then, we must include the polarity of whatever quality and direction our reaction is taking to integrate the fragmentation. Eventually, we develop new skills that can detect even subtler nuances for more in-depth exploration.

In this book and my classes, I offer a variety of ways to recognize energetic patterns. With practice, you can master skillful methods of reconnecting with Divine Essence. For example, in a group meeting, you can learn presencing practices to become more aware and connect with the subtle essence of your soul. I call these ongoing sessions Gifts of Being.

Sometimes a person presents a concern that is so complicated and convoluted that perplexed looks flood the other students' faces. They seem to be asking, "What are you going to do with that?" At such times, someone will anxiously jump in, filling the space with suggestions and advice for how to fix the situation. Or, a kind of nervous clatter may erupt in the room like the clucking of hens spying a fox circling their pen.

Yet in no time at all––with the gentle reminder to bring the focus back to oneself . . .witness the other. . .wait patiently. . .and surrender to trusting the mystery to unfold naturally––a miracle occurs. This transformational process can seem like a death, because the form we began with no longer exists. On our own, we might stop short of resolution, get stuck with what to do next, or spin it 'round mentally to figure it out as we avoid getting close to no-thing. Therefore, we need the support of the teacher and power of the group's witnessing until we have developed compassionate tolerance and patience enough to presence, witness, accept, and surrender, free of judgment and the need to control the outcome. It took us a lifetime to lose our way, and it also takes time to regain the path and trust that we won't abandon ourselves.

Surrendering to the Mystery

In the next chapter, I introduce two processes in which to explore through inquiry the beautiful presencing practice that has been passed on from teacher to student since antiquity. But first let us appreciate the wonder of transformation expressed in the following poem by a student who is now able to presence on her own. She shares with us the universal metaphor of letting go in order to rebirth. We, like seeds and grains, benefit from a soaking process so the rough husk can soften and fall away. Once able to access nature's core aliveness, we more fully receive the enzymes and nutrients of these living foods. Likewise, as human beings in transformation, we benefit from steeping in the fluid *Grace* of our essential nature, allowing the shell of past conditioning, false beliefs, and dark misunderstandings to melt away so that we may directly access the nourishing vitality and pure nature of our *Soul*.

We die so that we might live

*We fly close to the sun
In a frenzy of passion, sadness, despair,
Whatever it takes to get us there.
And our husk
Begins to burn
And crack,
To dry out
And break.*

*And we come back from the sun
Looking pretty bad,
Pretty beat up,
And we don't feel so good either.*

*We see our shell, our husk
Looking so shredded,
And we wonder why we did it,
Flew so close to the sun,
Got so close that we came back unrecognizable.*

*We might stay that way for a while, sitting in the brokenness of that place,
The loss of that husk.
It once was so pretty after all,
And it never will be again...*

*But then we begin to realize that the husk is breaking off, slowly at
first
And then falling away in great chunks.
And underneath
Is a form that you don't recognize,
New, shiny,
Pink,
Vibrant and vibrating.
Your skin is glowing from the inside out.
You move, and it isn't a husk body moving anymore.
Your body is sinuous and fluid.*

*Your old hull had to come off and fall away
To allow for this new life to come through.*

*This new body, this new life...
This is a life to awaken to——
A life of mystery and discovery, because now you feel so much more
[because]
Your husk isn't protecting you anymore.*

*And even the air moving across your skin is sensual.
Light dances in waves upon surfaces,
And you see all the things that you were too busy to notice before,
No longer blocked by your old husk.
New beings without husks come toward you, vibrating
In the same way you are.
You feel them, their energies, their thoughts and emotions.
You Know them somehow.*

This life is a turn on.
Your whole being is alive with life.
You feel your thoughts and feelings change your body

as they change within your mind and heart.

And you begin to notice that they also change your environment.
This is a "responsive" reality, a thousand times more responsive than
the world you left behind along with your old husk.

You had to die, to come alive.

—— Heidi Jo[3]

There are so many gifts
Still unopened from your birthday,
There are so many hand-crafted presents
That have been sent to you by God.
The beloved does not mind repeating,
"Everything I have is also yours."
There are so many gifts, my dear,
Still unopened from your birthday.

—— Hafiz[1]

Chapter 17

The Alchemy of Inquiry and Love

To be in pure presence with oneself and with others is an act of love. As we develop sensitivity to the ever-present subtlety of our essential nature, we are growing our faculty to love unconditionally. The challenge is that while in a physical body living on earth, we are at effect of dual forces. At the same time, we are innately bestowed with God-given gifts, the essences of our soul. Each subtlety, each quality of essence is an integral aspect of the wholeness we are. And if we are willing to receive these gifts, we will in turn return to feeling unified and whole.

Our essences consist of various affections of soul, attributes coloring characteristics of our consciousness. I have shared with you several principles of these teachings along the way. Now I'd like to bring them together to demonstrate how they apply when attending to a concern, such as in the following two examples that students brought to class.

In the following question-and-answer dialogue, the first participant shares her interest of concern. She is visibly agitated, and I guide her through the process:

Student (S) – *I've heard that if a soul doesn't behave, God can annihilate it from existence. If we are not good, we can disappear forever. That really scares me. I am always trying to be good, but I feel like I'm never going to be good enough for God. I'm afraid I will get punished because I will never be perfect enough.*

Kim (K) – *Are you open to bringing in curiosity and playing with this?*

S – *Yes.*

K – *What direction is the energy moving in your body when you think or say this?*

S – *Up.*

K – *To where?*

S – *My shoulders. But it goes up to my head. It's all pulled up.*

K – *What do you sense in your lower body?*

S – *Not much. It's pretty empty.*

K – *Does that feel safe?*

S – *No.*

K – *When you worry and feel afraid that you are being judged and doubt you will ever be perfect enough, where does that critical voice come from?*

S – *My head.*

K – *So the part of you that is determined to be perfect and punishes you lives in the head? So then who lives up above it all?*

S – *God.*

K – *Yes, according to this story! And what part of your personality is the punisher?*

S – *The criticizing part of my ego.*

K – *Yes, your superego. That self-critical voice, the admonishing part, the judge!*

Pause…

K – *Now what just happened in your body energetically as you realize this?*

S – *It relaxed. All the tension dropped down and released. I can breathe more fully now. I feel better.*

K – *Do you feel safe here?*

S – *Yes. I feel comfortable in my body. My mind feels at peace.*

Laughing...

K – So it appears that the story is nothing more than the self-critical aspect of the ego imitating the almighty, powerful God——a false god scaring you. This is a dominating, diminishing imposter of god rendering you powerless, persecuting you. Seeing the truth and trusting yourself is empowering, yes? When you reconnected with your inner guidance, the wisdom of that brought an essential quality of peace.

S - Yes. I trust myself. I feel safe, and it all makes me giggle!

Brilliant. You can see it is all right here, in full view, out in the open. But until we understand what we are looking at and the mechanisms at work, we get stuck in the convoluting loop of believing, avoiding, or becoming entangled in the lie. I'm going to break this down so that you can plainly see all of the principles at work.

As we step back through this particular process, we see that our student was innocently unaware that her sense of power was split off and projecting outward. In this case, above her was the commanding, demanding voice she interpreted as God. Her scary story about God was a perfect reflection resonating with her own self-critical internalized imposter of god, her superego——like the Wizard of Oz. Energetically speaking, she was feeling a separation between the above and the below, *heaven and earth.* Above felt intensified and below felt empty.

Telling Limiting Stories

What you have learned in the previous chapters is that the head has to do with thoughts and the story we tell ourselves——our beliefs. And the body houses instinctual drives toward or away from life. Any judgment creates a division between the mind and the body. This can show up as assumptions, criticism, prejudice, and more. It is what we refer to in this methodology as "splitting" or "separation." When this happens, limiting thoughts become like a demi-god, enforcing fear over the land of our body.

On one hand, when we connect the dots, we become aware of our brilliancy, the embodied realization of the light of our being. In other words, the brilliancy of our essence connects anywhere we have been disconnected, bridging the chasm.[2] When this integration occurs, we can feel the natural presence of essential empowerment as a larger version of ourselves, a bigger "I." The power simply IS; it is egoless with no effort involved. As a result, trust is natural because everything is lit up, out in the open, in full view.

On the other hand, when we operate from a limited view—the separation caused by preference, criticism, and judgment—we diminish our being and then project our power outward unconsciously onto any authority—be it God, the government, society, our parents or partners, the weather, or whatever or whomever we imagine is more powerful than we are. In this way, we maintain our persecution and victimization, even our superego! We remain infantile under the tyranny of our internalized superior critic and get to be right about everything that is wrong in our world. In the end, we deny responsibility for our part in being unconscious, which reinforces our powerlessness and paranoid thinking. We thus use our brilliance against ourselves, which is at the root of so much suffering.

Melting False Structures

If you remember from chapter 1, as long as the mind perceives itself as superior to and separate from the body, it believes it will escape annihilation. Unbeknown to the ego, however, annihilation is nothing more than the melting down of a false structure. This meltdown is actually the head joining the heart . . . fragmented parts of self that are returning and morphing back into the luminosity of embodied wholeness. In so doing, we are cultivating the humility to see that neither the limited mind nor our body is all we can be. Thus, we learn to trust our brilliance, which reconnects us to wholeness. When we are directly connected to our true self, we are also connected with the larger support of Source.[3]

Imagine what our world could be like if each one of us were to harness the runaway momentum of separation, which is nothing more than a fear-based sense of deficiency dedicated to maintaining the survival of an undeveloped identity from the past, right here. In all of ten minutes of presencing, the student in our example shifted her ground of reality. We have infinite opportunities daily to access and return to our fullness. And if we learn to discern the differences between the cleverness of mental mindscapes and that of Source brilliance, and practice returning to and claiming in an embodied way our wholeness, we can develop more ease and resiliency, which leads to our autonomy and capacity to live the fullness of life!

Is this what Einstein meant when he said that we use only ten percent of our brain? We use only ten percent of the intelligence available to us? Yet if we pay attention to, attend to, and occupy our mind-body connection, all three intelligence centers naturally line up: the mental, the emotional, and the physical. We return to balance, and we feel whole. Through experiencing our wholeness along with another, effortless reconnection occurs. Naturally this allows for even more connection leading our soul to connect with the Soul of Source––the micro and the macro in union!

Presencing is the practice of returning again and again, turning back to where we have come from, marrying the edges, expanding our view.

This brings us to the divine correction that happens when we realize our part in the creation of separation. Once the student in our example realized the trickery of how she had bought into the distortion of her old mind, her identity shifted from the impression of feeling inadequate to that of being whole, thus transforming the feeling of anxiety and self-deprecation to feeling peaceful and full. Had you been in the room to witness this shift, you may have felt the permeable, peaceful presence of quietude imbued by her essence. There was a penetrating sense of trust as she embodied the essential quality needed to heal the affliction of her limited thinking.

Such potency is the elixir of our soul, available to us once an alchemical transfiguration occurs—when truth exposes the chasm we have erringly created in ignorance. Turning at this choice point, we instead surrender to the wisdom of the mystery of that which has been unknown to us and wait for it to be revealed.[4] When we stop interfering and let go of our resistance, baring the light of consciousness in this manner, we are evolving the original concept of the story that has been passed down from generation to generation. Does this sound familiar? The sins of the father are passed down to the son, just as the sins of the mothers are passed along to their daughters.

Sin simply means that we have missed the mark! We missed the point! And the point is our True Self. When we catch ourselves in the act and are willing to expose what we don't know, a kind of magical alchemy appears. In other words, we realize a rendering of our old self into a new form.

Over time, we discover that as long as we criticize any limitation, we are in fact not only reinforcing but also re-creating the pain of our limited identification. This is why realization——*shining the light of truth*—— is not a one-time experience but a lifelong relationship of co-creative inter- and intra-connectivity. As we all know, we can't just exercise once and expect to stay fit. Our muscles will atrophy without use. To have awareness, we must exercise our perceptual muscles or slip back into the function of the lower mind. By surrendering to *not knowing while being finely focused*, we can hold with loving kindness and care the vulnerability of the innocence of what is undeveloped in us. Thus, we receive what we have longed for——the objective awareness of nonjudgment.

Illuminating What We Don't Know

Contrary to what we might think, essential objectivity is not cold and aloof, but rather all-inclusive and connecting. What we "don't know" is both exposed and received. Being present with this aspect of self is to be in loving presence with our innocence. Thus we are cultivating genuine acceptance for that part that didn't know any other way. That part didn't know any better how to be, not yet understanding that it is neither bad nor wrong to be who we are essentially. Yet through exposing the fuller truth, we can come to terms with any consensus we have had to bear because of our or another's shortcoming. From a larger view arises loving kindness and compassionate ease in the undoing of whatever it has been that we have done to others, or others have done to us. But ultimately, we get to see that the bigger truth is about what we have done to ourselves.

This brings us to the sacred chamber of our heart, referred to as the treasure in the heart or the golden locket of our innermost pure

Self––the Beloved. This place reflects our heart of hearts, illuminating the meeting of ego and essence coming together to evolve our personality in relation to our soul. It is here that our lives take a radical turn. We move from a multitude of projections to a life of gratitude for receiving the ever-present, ever-nourishing Grace streaming from the nectars of light and radiance that unfold our whole heart of being. Only from our soul can we receive and embody this *Divine Elixir* where...

> *Giving is receiving and receiving is giving through the*
> *infinite generosity of Divine abundance and goodwill.*

The next example illustrates how these same principles can be applied even when the issues of concern, outcome, and quality of essence are very different.

A person in the group is feeling the pang of the ending of a relationship, which is not her choice. The partner is not interested in closure and has become involved with a new romance. She shares her painful situation and remarks that all she ever wanted was a loving relationship and a family home. As she accepts her sadness, anger arises with a feeling of pressure and heat. This sensation builds when she touches into a sense of betrayal. I ask her to notice the energy of her emotions and to share what appears in her awareness.

As this person sits with the discomfort of her hurt, she can feel heat emanating from her body. In her mind's eye, she sees an image of the energy sparking in radiating rays. Now she perceives something at the end of these rays that look like little barbs. She realizes how enraged she really feels. As she is present with this rage, she shares that it is very uncomfortable here. I give her the option to step back. She pauses and now wants to continue.

While she is presencing the building velocity of emotion without acting it out, I assist her in breathing it through with the four-square breath (chapter 5). She shares that a shift is occurring and that now her core feels empty and cool.

"Interesting that your energy is moving out and away, but there is nothing here for you. What else do you notice?" I ask.

Sadness arises, and she is aware of her longing for the other. Every part of her is aching to reach out, wanting connection (which reveals the separation). As she stays present with the enormous charge and tolerates the energy, she becomes aware that the more she wants "what's out there," the emptier she feels inside. I remind her of the directions she is working with here, forward and back (future and past), and I ask her to rest back into the emptiness. She includes the emptiness and pauses, seeing a picture of herself as a child curled up into herself all alone. She is home alone and nobody is there for her. She feels loss and is at a loss to know what to do.

I reflect that no one outside of herself can fill this emptiness. Instantaneously, she gets it that now she is the one who is abandoning herself. I ask what would happen if she allowed herself to receive the rays. Her inner landscape reveals a picture of herself as a child in a sunlit meadow of flowers. She allows herself to receive the warmth of this nurturing aspect of nature and beauty. A kind sweetness fills her core. I notice a palpable shift in her, in the field of the room, and among all of us. Faces are glowing, hearts are flowing, and a preciousness and juiciness fill the air.

"What are you noticing?"

She responds with twinkling delight and the sweetest smile that she feels cozy, cared for, and filled with the warmth of contentment. She is detecting a honeyed-like substance, delicious and pure.

Her final response is, "I feel home."

Coming Home

Coming home is returning to the place where that wounded part of us, so very young and pure, has hidden our preciousness, our dearest most inner true self. Through all manner of defenses, we have barricaded and obscured this precious treasure, our essential identity, within our heart of hearts in a sacred chamber. To reach this is a most tender and courageous act. Coming home to our real self is honoring this gift of our being, unconditionally, whether anybody else does or not. Thus, the pain of our separation can heal. We cannot underestimate the profound effect this kind of practice can have on evolving our consciousness. Yet it is not as easy as it looks, until it is! In the meantime, we must continue to show up to re-awaken the amnesia 'til we no longer forget what we are. And in so doing we arrive.

In his book *The Station of No Station*, Sufi scholar Henry Bayman brings the message of faith and hope from the heartland of Central Anatolia, teachings of the great Sufi masters who introduce the most sublime states of consciousness. One such sharing is on the topic of what he calls *spiritual embryogenesis*.

To 'die' before you 'die' is to be born again. Hence one who has 'awakened'——in the presence of the term——is twice-born. Birds too are twice-born. In its first birth, the bird consists of an egg. If it is not reborn, leaving its shell behind, it can never fly.... The deepest and most profound core of all esoteric teachings has been reserved for the 'child of spirit.' In Sufism it is called the Child of Meaning {tifl al-maani} or Child of Heart {walad al-qalb}....

[T]he child grows. It passes through childhood and youth. The son of the Buddha grows up to inherit the Diamond Body of the Buddha. The star-child grows up to become the Superman. The Child of the Heart ascends to become the Perfect Human.... He needs to pass beyond the corporeal world to the spiritual world——the Secret World. Nothing exists there except the Essence of God. This is the infinite expanse where the child of meaning takes flight. There it sees strange and wonderful things, but it is impossible to convey information about them to others. This is the station of the People of Unity, who have found extinction {fana} from their own existence. Jesus has said: "Unless a man is born again, he cannot enter the Kingdom of God."[5]

SPIRITUAL HUNGER

Spiritual hunger is a living, radiant fire put by God into the Hearts of his servants so that their ego can be burned; when it has been burned, this fire then becomes the fire of longing, which never dies, either in this world or the next.
There is no quicker way to God than spiritual hunger; if it travels through solid rock, water gushes forth. Spiritual hunger is essential for the Sufis; it is the showering of God's mercy on them.

—— Abu Sa'id Abu'l Kheyr[1]

Chapter 18

The Essential Fairy Tale

The *Wizard of Oz*[2] is the quintessential story of spiritual hunger and the burning desire to return home. Our tale begins with Dorothy dreamily gazing far off into the sky, singing,

Somewhere, over the rainbow, way up high
There's a land that I heard of once in a lullaby.

Somewhere, over the rainbow, skies are blue,
And the dreams that you dare to dream really do come true.

Someday I'll wish upon a star
And wake up where the clouds are far behind me.
Where troubles melt like lemon drops
Away above the chimney tops,
That's where you'll find me.

Somewhere over the rainbow, bluebirds fly.
Birds fly over the rainbow,
Why then, oh why can't I?

If happy little bluebirds fly
Beyond the rainbow,
Why, oh why, can't I?

——Harold Arlen, "Somewhere Over the Rainbow"

This song describes a spiritual quest——a burning desire with longing in the soul to actualize the existential dream of *wishing upon the star*. Thus, Dorothy claims and lives the authentic expression of her essential identity. Self-realized, she awakens to embody the rainbow essences of her soul. She is *high above the chimney tops*, rising above limiting structures and clearing her mind from the clouds of confusion. She merges into the expansive spacious quality of sky-like openness, *where the bluebirds fly*. Her spirit is set free to open to new discoveries and the possibilities of her dreams, where *like lemon drops,* she melts into the sweetness of returning home to the precious nature and child-like wonder of her being.

Ultimately, we will all discover that home is not a land or a place far away. Home is where the heart is. With a click of her sparkling ruby slippers, which denote the autonomy of her *red essence*, she does not fly away in the balloon with her alter ego, the Wizard of Oz, but instead follows Toto (her intuition) to Oz, where the wizard is none other than the deficient identity formed in childhood hiding in the tower of the mind. This programmed state (exaggerated in the Wizard) cleverly fools others through self-importance and unreasonable demands in a pale imitation of Source.[2]

It is interesting that *oz* is an abbreviation for the water measure of ounces. And remember that water represents the vulnerability of any false structure built up by the ego. This thought brings us to the Wicked

Witch of the West, who terrorizes Dorothy and her companions to gain the slippers. The slipper is the soul. It is a perfect fit and cannot be removed, for it is mingled with the flesh. In the movie, the ruby red color of the slippers has a particular essence, mimicking the ruby channel of the soul. *Ruh* in the Qur'an is the vital fire of essential passion that animates our very aliveness. It is the ecstatic life force enlivening our body as it directly experiences the pure light of our soul. This leads to the journey of transcendence as we grow our capacity from one form to another. Students of this work will recognize the symbolism here of the fleshy pearl, the pomegranate essence.

Was it a purely cosmetic accident that inspired screenwriter Noel Langley to pick ruby red over the white silver corded slippers that the original author, L. Frank Baum, intended? Or was he guided by a mystical hunch that was ripe for the time? Indeed, he was witness to several impassioned acts that defined stepping out into a new frontier that were changing history at that time, such as Gandhi's revolutionary Salt March, the discovery of Pluto, Amelia Earhart's one woman flights, and World War II. But let's also take a look at Baum's choice of white and silver shoes.

In this work, white portrays the container that holds all parts of the whole. As the personality becomes more integrated, more embodied essentially, and more mature, one develops what is referred to as the pearl. The essential quality of the pearl is the ability to grow one's integral capacity of wholeness and resiliency. Whether it is red or white, the slipper denotes a stage of growth that requires a felt sense of integration and individuation––soul to soul, heart to heart. The silver cord is the connectivity of our brilliance, and the cord is often the symbol connecting us to the Great Mystery beyond physicality––above and below, heaven and earth.

Returning to the witch, we note that our villain retorts that the only way to separate Dorothy from the ruby slippers is to kill her. Possessed by jealousy and hatred, the witch will do whatever it takes to get those shoes, which symbolize the ability to walk in the world, to stand on one's own two feet. Dressed in black, the witch is a display of the perverted distortion of power. When in balance and her pure essential form, she is the seer, the magician, the shaman. Turning instead to deception and trickery, she becomes cruel and inflated, attacking at every chance.

Does this sound familiar? The witch is our superego, the internalized, unrelenting, admonishing critic who reacts defensively against feeling the core wound of her vulnerability, as we can see by the putrid green cast of her skin. She is green with envy and insanely hurt over the fact that her sister is more liked than she. The original story describes the wicked witch with a patch over one eye, showing us her inability to see the bigger picture. Her view is impaired by blinding hate to circumvent the void that her inflated personality has created. She is consumed with survival terror, the narcissistic wound of an early pattern laid down due to lack of intimacy with a caring parent in early infancy.

And what does Dorothy do to protect herself? She throws a bucket of water on the wicked witch. The entire kingdom stands witness as our villain dissolves, absorbed by a pool of liquid. The false structure has been annihilated, extinguishing the duality of the pain of separation between the Witch of the West and her sister, the Witch of the East, on whom Dorothy's house would fall. This symbolizes the perpetrator and the victim, the good one and the bad one, a split in the personal identity between the ego and the superego. The split reveals the innocent undeveloped aspect of the little "i" of the ego and the attacking superego of the critic, the punishing and demanding demi-God. All that is left of her is nothing——nothing save a piece of cloth. *Suf* from *Sufi* means "cloth of wool." Now we can see what occurs when a fallen, runaway ego makes the turn toward the One, the true identity of the enlightened Self. By integrating the undifferentiated power of Source, it is no longer split off and brandished as a weapon by the punishing self.

Our story started in Kansas, a gray and bleak land that represents the dull, ordinary world of mundane reality. When Dorothy returns to Kansas at the end of her quest, she finds instead a land that is fertile and flourishing with the colorfulness of life. Humbled by what it means to be a real human being, connected with others and united, she remembers the specific qualities of love and support provided by friends and family. All parts of self, all members, are now connected, allowing Dorothy to feel the integrity and wholeness of being her true authentic Self.

In Kansas, Dorothy was distressed over her little dog Toto. He had been taken by the sinister Miss Gulch, who is rigidly attached to the rules of society. Mean-hearted and judgmental, Miss Gulch is the real-life Wicked Witch of the West, representing the linear and calculating left brain. When Toto escapes from Dorothy's basket and runs away, we discover that although he can be restrained, he cannot be contained. Toto symbolizes Dorothy's instinctual intuition, her right-brained self. Throughout the story, we hear Dorothy talking to Toto (her intuitive self). Repeatedly, Toto is captured, hides, or runs away, but he always escapes his captors (the limited mind) and returns. Each adventure leads Dorothy to a better situation and ultimately transformation.

When along comes a tornado, she and Toto get inside the house (the box of mental limitations, representing Dorothy's fearful mind of the past) just in the nick of time for it to be lifted up and carried away in the momentum of the twister. Chaotically spinning 'round in the sky (much like the trauma vortex that comes with loss of identity and the dissociation that perpetuates fear and the energetic feeling of spiraling out of control), these two are in a place where there is no ground. Dorothy is up in her head and has no felt sense of being in the body.

They are carried off far away to a fantasyland. It is here where the house comes crashing down, landing on the Witch of the East and killing her. All that we see of her are, sticking out from beneath the structure, black-and-white striped stocking legs with the ruby slippers on her feet. Thus, the subconscious is hidden beneath what is conscious, and the mind is split in the duality of black-and-white thinking, Arriving just then is the feared witch, who is outraged at what she sees. Without remorse, her greedy self immediately reaches out to grab the slippers. It is all about her, and no one else matters; she is the center of her convoluted uni-verse! It is survival at all costs, demonstrated by her protruding head and beady eyes, the tell-tale signs of sympathetic overdrive.

Enter Glinda, who is the Guidance of unconditional love dressed in a billowy soft gown of pale pink and white, overlaid with the gossamer silver brilliancy of connectivity. Hers is an all-inclusive universe, the star of light, the Light of Source. She is the most powerful sorceress of Oz, and with an effortless wave of her wand, Glinda the Good (a kind and fair witch acting as a composite of the north and the south, heaven and earth) transfers the ruby slippers to Dorothy's feet. They fit her so perfectly that they cannot be removed, which is akin to the soul's ecstatic expression of life and love for its body. Once again Dorothy is invited to follow the passion of her burning desire to find a way home. The wicked witch curses Dorothy and threatens to make her life miserable till she gets her sister's ruby slippers back—the enchanted slippers of the divine beauty of the soul.

One by one, the munchkins appear, coming out from behind the trees and flowers. They signify the pure natural preciousness of being. As a child we learned to hide our precious nature, the sparkling essences of soul within the secret sacred chamber of our heart of hearts, to protect who we are so that no one could find us or harm us here. The munchkins welcome Dorothy and light her way on the path to returning home. Song and fanfare arise with all kinds of celebration as they exclaim, *"Follow the yellow brick road!"* The yellow brick road is the path of inquiry. It is the curiosity and innocence of the child's mind joined with the fluidity of a joyful heart and the freedom to be who we are naturally.

Dorothy eventually arrives at a crossroad, confused as to which way to go. While talking aloud to herself and Toto, she hears someone give directions. Astonished, she looks around and sees no one, until it becomes clear that the voice belongs to a scarecrow. He is the first of three characters she meets along the path to Oz.

Thus begins her spiritual journey to discover the essential nature of the three intelligence centers: the mind represented by the scarecrow, the heart represented by the tin man, and instinct represented by the lion. Each of them cries a song of woe concerning the particular ailment of the deficiency from which they believe they suffer. Together they decide that the Great Wizard of Oz can help them. Arm in arm they set off together to find the Emerald City, a land of healing, where they hope to meet the Great Oz in his beatific castle so that they can return home. The palace is the citadel of truth and the emerald represents the jewel in the heart of compassion. It is a place of loving-kindness and healing of every kind.

Each of our characters' fears represent a precise defense tactic specifically related to their particular center. The scarecrow loses his ground when the monkeys pull out his stuffing, leaving him with only a talking head and no connection to his body. And when crossing the river, he gets so impatient that he tries using a pole to force forward the boat, which ends up getting stuck in the mud, leaving him high and dry, abandoned, and alone as the others drift away. Through trials and tribulations, the scarecrow learns to face his fear of not knowing and to bow his head to his heart because the head can't do it alone. As he learns to trust the guidance of heart and follow his gut along with the wisdom of his brain, the bigger plan unfolds.

Next we follow the tin woodsman, who has accidently cut off different parts of himself over the heartache of his lost love. His loss is due to a spell cast upon his axe by the Wicked Witch of the West. Saddened, he goes to a tinsmith asking to create a body of metal to further separate him from feeling his hurt. Now all that can be felt of his heart is a hollow place. Metal armor is a defense against feeling emptiness. Again and again along their journey he is tested with selfless acts of love to save his companions from the perils of the witch. Each loving act of kindness leads to deeper and deeper feelings of love and compassion for himself as well as the others. Eventually, his emptiness vaporizes as he becomes full and loving and juicy.

Last, we have the cowardly lion. To defend himself against feeling inadequate for his lack of courage, he compensates by intimidating and bullying others. Underneath it all, he feels he doesn't have what it takes to be in his wholeness. He contains no real substance and bolsters himself up with a blustery attitude that covers mere puffed air. As a result, he suffers from an extreme lack of confidence. In the story, he is asked to face his fear and demonstrate that he is in fact courageous. Our lion-hearted one develops his capacity by showing consistent loyalty and reliability. This willingness supports a rooted sense of integrity and being grounded to fully inhabit his body.

Once the river is crossed and our friends have reunited, they come upon a vast field of oriental poppies they must pass to reach the palace. This is a spell cast by the witch to prevent them from reaching Oz. The sedative power of the opiates takes hold, and they fall into a deep sleep, unconscious of the reality ahead that they must face. The drowsy sleep is a perfect defense against awakening from the story of the past and moving beyond their fears. Seeing their plight, Glinda casts her own spell, a powdery soft snowfall to awaken our travelers. This fresh perspective brings with it sobriety and support for what needs to be done. Each one has to rally, lifting himself out of a stupor to go beyond what he has previously known.

At last, our heroes arrive at the gates of the Emerald City, where they are ushered into enchantment and splendor. Attendants refresh them, and they rest for the night before meeting the Great Oz. The next day, they are taken to his chamber, where they anxiously await him. Told that no one has ever seen him, they realize a mystery is about to unfold. Next, they are met with terrorizing images. Each one sees what he fears most. They are told that if they want to get what they desire, they must obey his commands. Oz tells Dorothy she must kill the witch and bring him her broom as proof.

When the four companions return with the broom, Oz keeps putting them off. Eventually, they take a stand and enter his domain. They are met by the Great and Terrible Oz doing his best to scare them away. Amid this tirade, Toto pulls back the curtain, revealing a tiny man pulling levers and turning dials in the theater of his small room. Oz is not the great wizard they and the entire kingdom had thought. He is nothing more than a petty tyrant, an imposter putting on a show. In fact, he is a balloonist who was performing a circus act when he and the hot air balloon had been swept away. He dropped down in a land where the inhabitants had not seen anyone like him before. They made him the wizard and ruler of their land. Taken by flattery, he went on living the lie of his true identity.

Seeing the forlorn look of disappointment upon the faces of our foursome, Oz gives each of them a trinket as a condolence to symbolize their success. But for Dorothy, he builds a hot air balloon and will personally take her back to Kansas. Just as the balloon sets off, Toto jumps out. Dorothy chases after him and watches the balloon fly away without her. Yet hers is the realm of essence; it doesn't constitute matter. She is encouraged by the inhabitants of Oz to seek the good witch Glinda, who tells Dorothy that the slippers she wears, her very soul, have had the magic to take her home all along. All that she needs to do is click her heels three times, bringing together the three centers for her return.

In Hebrew the word *Oz* implies strength, and as denoted by the red shoes, Dorothy must now draw upon her own inner strength if she wants to return home. All along she has been navigating the edge of strength and vulnerability, evolving her relationship to Self. A variation of the name *Dorothy* means "gift of God," suggesting the fall from Grace and the return that must be made to find one's way back to Unity.

For Dorothy's is the path of the mystic, and the scripture of the mystic is to experience human nature. To be free, she must develop the capacity to see the point of view of each person. She must know the constellation of all the characteristics of her internal world as well as an external worldview. She must be able to openly see the reason behind all reasons, bridging the heart of the matter. She needs to see into the very essence of others' lives, and to view her life from an open, unprejudiced stance of unconditional love. Recognizing that the body and mind are vehicles through which the soul can experience life, so begins one's journey toward immortality.[4]

There are many more fairy tales such as this that find their roots in the mystical teachings of the Sufis. The Grimm brothers borrowed from the wisdom stories as did Chaucer and Shakespeare, and there can be endless interpretations to each. Here I have combined elements from both the *Wizard of Oz* book written by L. Frank Baum (1900) and the popular movie (1939). Baum was not only a member of but also the newspaper editor for the Theosophical Society. He no doubt gleaned rich metaphors there for the inner reality that he vividly illustrated in his stories.

There are numerous accounts of the archetypes according to Carl Jung, but here I have focused primarily on the esoteric, psycho-spiritual qualities of essence from the Oz story that have to do with *latifas* as described in Faisal's teachings, known as the ninety-nine names of God ~ Allah, which I have interpreted to translate this story. Both ways are complementary to each other and at the same time unique, and the core message rings clear through and through. This is a story of liberation and transcendence.[5] In the beginning, Dorothy seeks the answers outside of herself. In the end, she must turn toward and trust the Guidance within, and no one can do it for her. Likewise, the teacher can point the way, but we alone need to take the steps to becoming whole.[6]

What fairy tale character are you? What story is most like your story? Mine was Cinderella. As the eldest child, I had more chores and responsibilities than my two younger stepsisters. I felt hurt when they got more goodies than I did. So I resigned myself to the orphaned servant identity. As in the Wizard of Oz, there is also a special slipper in the Cinderella story. It is a glass slipper, representing the clarity of basic reality. This suggests that I am supported no matter what, healing my fear of confrontation and punishment. I had to walk this path to undo the powerlessness I felt and awaken to the stability and support of an infinite sustainer of All—Source.

Are you the royal prince saving damsels in distress? Or, the knight in shining armor who gets the castle and all its riches? Perhaps you are Little Red Riding Hood, betrayed by the deceptive antics of those you most trusted, or the Sleeping Beauty whose consciousness is awakened by a kiss. Whatever your character, here lies a template to look at all parts of yourself. In the end, like Goldilocks we discover *enough*. By cherishing the enoughness of "just right," we find comfort in the little things of life, the simple pleasures and subtle nuances of what it is to be an essential human being.

The power of the fairy tale colors all of our lives with the myth and magic of an essential story waiting to be claimed. I was once just like Dorothy,[7] who at the age of 12 (when transforming from a child to an adult) took her first step of renewal. My parents created the Children's Little Theater in our community. Mom designed the costumes and sets, and Dad constructed them. My sisters and I performed in the productions. Our whole family was involved. Being the shy one, I often had a dance piece and was rarely asked to speak. Yet I had one bit part that was a match—Scheherazade. I was to introduce the story before the play began.

Here I am standing in front of the curtain before it opens, dressed in a golden sari with a jewel over my third eye. I am looking out over the expanse of the theater in a faraway gaze to deliver this message: "In the antiquity of time, in ancient Persia, there lived a King. And the King had a son...," so the story continued.

This was my first stage experience in feeling a total state of Oneness with the audience. And it was that heightened, enlightening experience of Unity that propelled me into the performing arts. The difference that day was that I got out of my own way.

I would like to see in temples and churches souls with real spirituality according to my standard. Spirituality is spirituality. I mean more than the goodness in souls who are living according to certain moral and spiritual principles. I mean actual contact of God. That is my idea of spirituality.

—— Paramahansa Yogananda[1]

Chapter 19

Consciousness, Gnosis, and Witnessing

To recognize our true nature, *our essence,* we need to develop a discriminating capacity to tell things apart, and this process can take time. First, we hear about a mysterious Light. Then, we begin to see the Light in others in all manner of ways. Next, we recognize that this Light is in us. Finally, we have direct experience of the Light that we *Be.* The following are the stages of *gnosis,* with "it" being the Light of God:

> *I hear about it ~ I see it from afar ~ I have an experience of it ~ I am it! ~ And beyond...*

There are many traditions, religions, and spiritual schools of consciousness and enlightenment. All have a wealth of teachings to share, and many have in common the ancient mystical awakening process of gnosis, self-knowing. The sacred methodology of gnosis that I teach comes via the historical wisdom teachings and spiritual philosophy of Pir-o-Murshid Hazrat Inayat Kahn. In a recent book titled *Caravan of Souls,* his grandson, Pir Zia Inayat-Kahn, has compiled teachings of his grand-father and others who were torchbearers of illuminated knowledge. The following stages are prefaced by my simple paraphrasing of his master-ful contribution to humanity:[2]

1. The first stage has to do with seeing the world through the temporal senses of our material body. Coming from this reality, it appears that what we see, hear, smell, taste, and feel prove that this particular plane of consciousness exists.

   ~ Here one learns about a higher conscious, God.

2. The second stage goes beyond the five basic senses and works through the mental plane. This is a higher perceptual conscious-ness. Here a person is deeply absorbed in his subject though contemplative thought and imagination.

   ~ Here one realizes that God is not only in heaven, but is on earth, too.

3. The third stage involves a mystical experience of consciousness. It is like being in a sound sleep yet wide awake. Often a person experiences God within, bringing joy, peace, and well-being. The subtle organs of the soul are active here, as are the higher mind and imaginal world.

   ~ The seer feels the presence of God and recognizes his divine Beloved in everyone in every form.

4. The fourth stage is beyond the material plane. It is diving into our deepest self-hood, touching our deepest being, the home of all intelligence. Here there is no fear or death. There is greater joy and peace, deepening into the divine.

   ~ God is realized. The language of words are subtle and silent, too vast to express.

5. The fifth stage is merging with God, at-one-ment.
   ~ *There is no longer an "I" or a "you." All Is.*

This brings us to the fact that before spiritual awareness can become self-actualized, we need to see the ways in which we continue to act out the belief that our conditioned identity is who we are.[3] We must expose any part of us that still sees our soul as separate, as something out there to go to, be channeled, or obtained. For we have yet to recognize the nascent immediacy of being, the constancy of now-ness. Soul doesn't leave us. It is we who disconnect.

Learning a New Language

We are learning a new language, the language of being, and there are not a lot of words with being. Whatever words exist are more spacious yet precise, fuller yet more empty, compact yet more open. The simple practice of observing our words teaches us the value of simply showing up and being here. *Being* is value.

Thus, being present allows for a larger perspective. From this larger view, we are able to witness all parts of the whole to the best of our ability. The witnessing Self[4] is more expansive than that of the personal "I." This perspective is organic, natural, and all inclusive, giving room to the ebb and flow of any insecure thoughts of not doing enough, doing it right, or that it should have been done already. We are exposing the split between *doing and being*. Here we find that the less we do, the louder the protest of "I." So we learn to include the insecurity of the *should*s in the full presence of being. We let it all come up and let it all go to the constancy of the enoughness of what is much larger. We are not trying to get rid of anything, just allowing it all to be here, simple, and pure.

> *What is asking to be seen? Don't fight the sleepiness, the dullness, the lead. Let yourself go under. Just be with it, floating in the sea ~ the mist ~ holding on to nothing ~ just floating. This is enough. Feel your soft rhythmic breath, touching the depth of your awareness ~ sky-like openness. Cast your net into the sea, not knowing what will come of it. There is no force, no insistence, just letting yourself flow with the current. You have full open awareness as you rest in the gentle caress and fluidity of liquid luminosity.*

Witnessing Begins Here

Witnessing begins right here in our own skin. All of our senses are included, inner and outer. Witnessing is a paradox, both local and nonlocal. There is a delicate balance in noticing "it all." Pure witnessing has nothing on it ~ nothing sticks ~ nothing is hidden. From this expansive view, we are seeing things as they are. We are seeing through the distortion all the way into the heart of the matter. Witnessing brings with it precision, like the three *C*'s of a priceless diamond—–the cut, the clarity and the color. Through the art of this mystery, we ask our mind to be pristine, cutting through any falsification of the truth. Now we can see into the situation with a clear, open focus.

Discriminating what is or is not wisdom needs to be an ongoing practice. It requires that we hold our awareness, attending to the edge of reciprocal dynamic tension, much like the fusion in nature that forms the diamond. The diamond grows while under the pressure and friction of forces both internal and external.

Yet the harder we actually try, the more we block objectivity. In truth, witnessing (without overstepping into tension) opens doors to the bigger picture, bringing insight to what was in plain view but could not yet be seen.

The power of witnessing is illustrated in the following account of my meeting with a student. He came feeling disappointment about the bickering of his colleagues and the strife of disconnect he was experiencing at his workplace.

Here is what his soul gifted him with:

Perceiving his work from open, expanded awareness, the student has both a felt sense of his situation and this vision...

He lets himself go... landing with a heavy, weighted sensation in his body. Energetically descending, he finds himself sinking in dense heavy mud. His form is dissolving. A stream appears, and he realizes that he is a fish. He finds himself swimming through the stream out into the open water... A man cups the fish up into his hands. He brings it up to his mouth and swallows it. The fish is now in the man's belly... The student looks at the man, and he sees himself.

His countenance is now radiant, glowing in a field of nondual unity. He is at peace with the profound interconnection that his being has provided[5]

Like the ouroboros, he released the entanglement of the past and moved into direct self-realization of inner selfhood, which is renewing and life sustaining.

Knowing Where We Are

Knowing where we are in relationship to witnessing is an important discernment. To the untrained initiate, the "watcher" and the "witness" can look alike. But these two states are very different, as is also the outcome. By discerning the look-alike activity of the ego's divisive imitation of witnessing, we find that the one who watches is looking only from the head and is personally invested. This watcher of our false self is the imitator. It uses whatever it sees as fuel, promoting only its own personal interest in a self-centered attempt to get what it wants by forcing its will. This self believes it is the center and controller of the universe. And whether it asserts its will through the grandiosity of being "better than" or "lesser than," or whether pendulating between both poles, the ego reveals its dual nature and limited identity. The watcher's view is narrow, closed-in as a result of judgment and a ridged stance. Marble eyes protrude, sprung from the acrid defense that is readied below tightened skin and shallow breath, brain stem clenched. The watcher looms in the shadows, shape shifting to avoid being detected by the witness self.

The witness is aware of the watcher, observing its erratic movement in the rat-maze labyrinth engineered by the mind. The witness offers asylum should the watcher fall through the membrane and into the infinite pool of vulnerability, dropping down deep to the dark underside. Here in the pond of awareness, where the unperceivable utterance can be detected, is the penetrating stillness of liquid light, a firmament where the two worlds meet––unconscious and conscious. A splash from above or below breaks through in brief moments to obtain life-giving oxygen. The all-pervasive brilliance penetrates, offering glistening beads along the murky reeds in the soft mud below and illuminating consciousness. A timeless sheen upon the mirror of this infinite horizon frees the lungs. Breath lets go...

Witnessing the Self

Oftentimes, one side of your nature will be conscious and the other unconscious. This is where the less-personal aspect of objective witnessing is helpful, for the witnessing self is a higher function of the pineal, your single all-seeing eye that bridges both personal and universal realities. Here your will is in step with God's Will, raising the lower functioning ego to a state of grace. It is imperative that your first practice be to witness yourself, your immediate world, and your interactions in relationships.[6] It is not about what others are doing. Focus instead on what *you* are doing. Notice your reactions and what you do with them. Do you suppress them, project them, get entangled in, or ignore them? Whatever you *do*, it is a defense.

By now we have discovered that our defenses, such as aggression, resistance, rejection, denial, self-hatred, and other types of acting out, make it difficult for us to be present with who we truly are. From this point of view, we are not yet awake to the fact that our reactions cannot be understood until we actually turn around and become aware of what we have split off. This means we need to recognize and perceive through a felt sense how this separation is due to our own ignorance. We simply didn't know or learn that any other way was possible.

Ignorance is learned. It is the way our ego develops in relationship to our environment and its unique flavors of pride, prejudice, superstition, and fear. Our family and society help to color our lens, and then it is up to us to see the bigger truth in a clearer way. We learn all kinds of views about reality, yet it is nothing more than *our* ideas about reality. For example, some people believe that war brings peace. Until they know differently, nothing can be said or done to dispel their myth. We must go directly to the heart of the matter. Often what we think something is about is not what is true at all.

Much of our conditioning is acquired the first few years following birth. That an individual's consciousness is already in effect at birth, and even prebirth, is a sobering idea. Thus, consciousness as a whole evolves slowly, with change occurring over innumerable generations. Indigenous wisdom teachings say that it takes seven generations to change or heal the past. It is a rare individual indeed who will manage to move beyond native conditioning. Yet it is possible through consciously exercising our choice. By fine-tuning our subtle organs of perception, growth can occur. Practice, patience, and perseverance plus plenty of rest to assimilate the changes offer a tried and true formula for success.

Learning With Kindness

As with a child, what is not learned needs to be taught. And when taught with kindness, as happens through the gentle nature of essence, one discovers that reactive defenses can dissolve, freeing us of their limitation. In place of the limitation, we experience illumination, shedding light upon what we have not yet seen and bringing more clarity and connection with our True Self.[7] This is like the experience I had when, at 18 years old, I endured strangulation and assault from a murderer who threatened to cut out my eyes. For years thereafter, I shuttered and couldn't allow myself to remember the sight of him. Then one day, I knew I had to move through this terror, allowing myself to see what I had so long been afraid of.

From my innermost eye, I gazed into the endless darkened well of his eyes. I saw there an innocent child, terrified, abused, and abandoned. He was wandering lost and alone in the night in lightless streets of prostitutes and pimps, needles and hate. Seeing who he was, which fostered such acts of cruelty, brought out an immense depth of compassion and love flooding my entirety. Brilliance ignited. Light was all I could see. He was a servant of God, and within him was the God he did not yet know. In that eternal instant of truth, all was understood and forgiven. The part of me that had not been embodied was now let free to feel again, and he was seen and released from the prison of my mind. A haunting nightmare from my past was over.

The storm had ended. The dull sleepiness that had overtaken me so that I wouldn't see lifted as the vast openness of consciousness washed clear my mind, relinquishing my lifelong fear of being seen. What I had most longed for as a child was also what I was always most afraid of. Now held, the All-pervading powerful Mystery enveloped me, permeating every cell of my being. Each cell was a cell in the heartbeat of God, amplifying sonic waves, rippling out all directions simultaneously. I felt imploding buoyancy, reformed anxiety rising up from below, supporting me in the infinity of All That Is ~ Illuminating the Way. The external and distant Light at the end of the tunnel was now internal, embodied as One.

This episode brought to resolution a long lost history fiercely tucked away in the recessed folds of my mind——of being left for dead as a preemie, shaken as a baby, and later near drowning, suffocation, and strangulation. I could not allow myself to see this shocking reality in its entirety before I was able to See. For without the witness, it is too devastating to be awake and can cause us more harm than good. Yet when the time arrives and we have developed the skillful means, we can then see the reason why we have come. It was at this moment that I remembered I had agreed to learn to understand what terror and panic and fear are, to fully Know the effects and the remedies for such profound spiritual considerations. It is through my journey of many years and years and years that I offer you these re-Sources...

When the chaotic momentum of panicked overwhelm is presenced and witnessed together at the same moment, it may feel equivalent to standing in a stormy wind while also feeling contained and in touch with oneself despite the fury. It is being steadfast and patient, resilient and strong while also interfacing with astronomical biodynamic pressure, the arrival of calm in the center of the cyclone. This is the tone when extreme fear is both presenced and witnessed simultaneously. During such times, one has the capacity to feel and intuit the intensity of the velocity along with sensing any opposite antidotal quality. In this case, calmness can collapse the force of duality. Self-realized, we return to a state of normalcy with an unequivocal sense of equanimity and rest—a great, natural deep peace.

Murshid's Blessing

May your heart be filled with heavenly joy,
May your soul be illuminated with divine light,
May your spirit uphold the divine Message,
May you go on in the spiritual path,
May God's peace abide with you forever and evermore.

—— Pir-o-Murshid Hazrat Inayat Kahn[1]

Chapter 20

Holy Here, Wholy You

Neither awake nor asleep, as if in a dream half remembered, we may linger in a realm where many truths are revealed. We find ourselves where land meets sea, exposing the porosity and Light of our immortal being. By drawing away the veils of illusion one after another, we arrive at a place most deeply hidden, at last to open our inner sight of truth. We now see that God was never hiding, has not abandoned us, nor was nonexistent. We discover that the distortion has been none other than ourselves, blinded by our own limited beliefs.

With the parting of each veil comes knowledge of a precise quality of essence to remedy our every ailment, reconnecting us through direct experience with soul.

What was darkness turns radiant, and new light brings secrets to the seer of Truth. The light that we have been seeking outside of us we find is already within. It has been lighting our way all along, illuminating everyone and everything in view. Each experience exposes a particular truth and essence of love. Eventually we turn inward toward the One––the Light of Guidance within our soul.

These subtle nuances of essence, like whispers, are easy to pass by with little notice or understanding until the clarity of our awareness penetrates through.[2] Like having a tongue dotted with undeveloped taste buds raised on artificial sweeteners, without the Light we cannot take pleasure in the bouquet of flavor ripe fruit offers. We will reject the sweet fruit in favor of bitter, refined sugar until we know any different.

The uniqueness of this teaching gives us skillful means by which we can learn to differentiate and discern the essential qualities of our authentic self that have gone undetected. For within each of us resides a precise landscape of pressurized, egoistic responses as well as the barely perceivable subtler terrain of our soul.

Presencing What Is Present

Presencing our energy and understanding what we perceive are skills we need to develop.[3] "What we see is what we get" at first glance is true. But what lies below can be quite the contrary, as when anger is masking sadness or when sadness masks frustration. If we run with the momentum of the emotion that is most obvious and forget to include the pause, which is the space providing for self-reflection to enlarge our view, we end up fortifying the defense and finding ourselves lost in a crazy land––just to keep from dropping in and meeting what is below that.

Yet each time we say "yes" to the invitation, no matter how pretty or profane, we accept the "choiceless" choice through our motiveless motivation. Thus, we both engage with and awaken to the fuller embrace of an unconditional loving Grace. The more we practice, the more we can feel and perceive other realms and dimensions of awareness.[4] Through every aspect of awakened perception, each glimpse is a precise teaching imparted from the Light of our Guidance to our ego. Thus, we heal any misunderstanding about "me" through the higher consciousness of unity. Here we can see that our original sin was not that we were lowly, unworthy, or impure. It was none other than the fact that we didn't know, whether through the purity of innocence, learned ignorance, or heedlessness. Now we have an opportunity to *know* differently if we so choose.

Through this knowing grows an outrageous gladitude and in-pouring gratitude, which at a certain point in our development will bring us to our knees. Here we bow our will to the Will of the Divine. We embody the heaven of our light in the earth of our body, healing the chasm between depression and ecstasy, fear and love, loss and intimacy.... In this way, we navigate the edge, bringing us home to fully claim and inhabit our life -force energy and unique way of being ~ being All that we are ~ living authentically our wholeness of being ~ a loving Light glowing through this mind, body, and soul.

Inspired by a third-year class, I now share this anthem:

Be original, be yourself, don't compare yourself to others. Have the courage to express your truth, even if it's not like another. Allow your tenderness to be seen; embrace the beauty of your strength. Discover the mystery that is hidden: your in-most wisdom, guidance, and grace. Allow for times of solitude to deconstruct what doesn't serve you. And dare to venture the vast unknown till you turn to face the light within you.

Honor the gift of life you've been given, no matter how difficult it may seem. For in the claiming of what is possible, new realities shall grow esteem. Appreciate your preciousness, whatever it may be, for it's not to judge yourself or others; it's to be nurtured and cultured by love and set free.

Awaken to the dream that dreamt you are possible and live responsible as uniquely you. For what is true is authentic, is whole undivided, is pure and sustainable, it's essentially you

To live authentically is to cultivate and value the preciousness of being that we truly are and to grow through love any part of self that doesn't yet know its genuine beauty.

In Love, Light, and Peace ~ Amen

Conclusion

Bringing It All Together

By now I trust you have taken note of a theme that runs throughout this book: *inclusion*. Attending to this primary principle with careful consideration grows the capacity to feel secure. Wholeness requires that you become aware of any reactivity arising from yourself or another. You are learning to notice energetically any place in which a reaction has occurred, thus exposing distractive tactics that may appear either consciously or unconsciously positioned to avoid what lies below. And what lies below—often a tangle of overwhelming emotions and sensations based on historical feelings of inadequacy—must eventually be met for the sake of becoming free.

While our defenses can offer temporary relief of anxiety, in the long run we risk disconnection from healthy relationships and insufficient stability to be present with reality. In contrast, the essential value of the *white latifa* is that wholeness holds it all! Easier said than done, however, for inclusion asks us to presence what we may not want to see, hear, or feel. Thus, it is important to have a personal inner practice, developing rough edges until we are strong enough to act effectively in the world.

This brings us to a valuable technique you can use to grow your skills: *titration*. Throughout this book, you are shown how to back up or come in for a closer look, titrating that edge. If you are swallowed in a vortex of reactivity, then catch yourself in the act while opening your awareness to include the bigger view. This allows for more objectivity. If you are spaced out, then find a focal point of awareness while noticing the tenacity of distractions that tempt––and keep bringing yourself back to the point. These are basic skills needed to traverse the terrain of the mind, the *black latifa*. You are loosening the grip of going into the rabbit hole. In time, discriminating wisdom and acuity of discernment will be yours as the chasm is absorbed into the full spectrum of the luminous midnight sun. As a result, you are empowering what has felt disempowered. Here resides deep peace, the serenity of quietude, and a safe haven of relaxation.

Layer after layer when uncovered reveals aspects of mistaken identity, showing us ways we have split from basic reality. While "peeling the onion," we will encounter whatever is needed to provide what feels supportive. When we open our heart to the reality of this truth, we become imbued with an essential love, a particular quality. Thus, a precise latifa is provided as the specific healing antidote to what we did not know how to create on our own. The healing is for the ego so that she may grow. Offered is an infinite provision, an unlimited supply to reconnect us with the essential Whole. I will delve into the realm of the latifas in my next book. But for now, it is important to learn the basic navigational skills of energetic movement and the profound effect of how something so seemingly simple can impact our psyche, emotions, and physical body.

Another valuable practice is *surrender*. Until we let go, we cannot know freedom. In his book *Tales of the Dervishes: Teaching Stories of Sufi*

Masters Over the Past Thousand Years, Indries Shah illustrates this point. He tells the tale of a hunter in "How To Catch Monkeys." The hunter knows that the monkey loves cherries, and so he places a cherry inside a narrow-necked bottle. Upon seeing this, a monkey comes down from a tree and reaches inside the bottle to grab the cherry. Holding tight to the sweet fruit, the monkey is unable to rid his hand from the bottle. Along comes the hunter to claim his prize, because the greedy monkey would not let go. As a result he could not escape. Thus the monkey lost his freedom.

The monkey and the hunter represent two sides of the same mind split apart. The monkey is the desirous mind that holds on to what it can't have. It wants what it wants even if it costs us our life. To a mind caught in the unconscious instinct for survival, letting go feels like it will die. Yet the irony is that this blind animal drive is actually a death wish. To surrender from here is the scariest step we will ever take, but it is in fact our liberation. The hunter's perspective, unlike the victim—survivor mentality of the monkey, represents the part of our mental structure that is cunning, looking for ways to entrap our innocence and ignorance. And so the split occurs——one side loving to persecute, and the other, to flagellate itself.

Are you starting to see the possibility of four directions of distortion——the above and below, the mind and the body? The hunter mind plays god, repressing our memories and tempting us with ob-jects we desire. We have forgotten who and what we really are. As we expose and sort out these distortions, both our mind and our body can rest, becoming more integrated and whole. This wholeness is our preciousness, to which no object can be compared. Now the higher mind of divine intelligence, the living source, can guide our way, and we may trust it.

Yet to convolute our separation from Self even more, we may experience a side-to-side pendulation, a "Dr. Jekyll and Mr. Hyde" scenario. This is like having two distinct personalities, or more if we become so identified. As we learn to trust we are safe in the unknown, the chasm or split in our personality further integrates. Now healthy, our ego serves the divine. These prior separations are fixed in time, based on the past and future––forward and back. The more present we become, the more this split comes together. Eventually, we experience the unity of no time. The object of our attachment is no longer someone or something out there. It is instead the marriage of Oneness between our essence and the divine.

Add into this mix the dynamics of expansion and contraction. Expansion is expressed as truth, contraction as untrue––the macro and micro, the cycle of life and death, birth and rebirth. As our barometer of perception becomes finely tuned and we align with what is true, we experience a more genuine quality of life along with more constancy and balance day by day. We now can trust that if we don't know how to do something, we can ask or learn. No longer is there the reactivity and desperate avoidance of shame, or feeling like it's the end of the world. As we mature in this way, we have more ease and resiliency in our special way of being in the world. We are loosening the grip of identifying with others' opinions in determining who we are. Here we can both cherish and understand that our uniqueness is essential in the balance of the collective whole.

We are free now. We are universal citizens, sovereign unto our Self. Each being is a uni-verse of I Am-ness, an instrument of the Divine. Our little mind has surrendered to the wisdom of the Great Mind, our will surrendered to Divine Will. Embodying heaven and earth, we are complete and whole. Only here can we experience true realization and actualization; only here can we Be free.

The following page offers a Quick Glance Reference Guide to chapters in this book where you can find exercises to support the steps needed to develop an energetic pathway to wholeness.

Quick Guide to Experiential Exercises

By simply engaging in these basic steps to embody energetic wholeness, you are empowering yourself to build a reliable foundation for life. This practice provides a consistent way to deepen your ability to

G ~ Grow confidence.

R ~ Raise consciousness.

A ~ Actualize your destiny.

T ~ Trust the truth within you.

I ~ Integrate and embody wholeness.

T ~ Turn toward oneness wherever you are.

U ~ Understand the nature of duality and unity.

D ~ Develop compassion for yourself and all others.

E ~ Empower new choices for being authentically you.

Love is our birthright. To align in truth allows us to actualize the essential love that we are blessed with innately. Dare to Be all you can Be!

Glossary

Achilles: the strongest and largest tendon in the body that pulls on the heel when the calf muscle flexes, allowing us the spring action to stand on our toes. It is also the weakest point, rendering it vulnerable to injury due to lesser blood flow and the excessive tension placed on it.

Adage: an old and well-known saying that expresses a general truth.

ADD: Attention deficit disorder, or attention deficit/hyperactivity disorder, is a brain-based syndrome that has to do with the faulty regulation of certain brain functions related to attention, concentration, memory, motivation and effort, learning from mistakes, impulsivity, hyperactivity, organization, and social skills.

Adrenals: endocrine glands that produce a variety of hormones, including adrenaline and the steroids aldosterone and cortisol. These glands are found above the kidneys.

Alchemy: a science and philosophy of transmuting one state to another, such as base metals into gold. Transmuting a dense substance into a subtle elixir, such as ignorance to wisdom.

Amrita: from Sanskrit, India: the nectar of immortality granted by God.

Amygdala: area of the brain that links strong emotions to experiences and memories.

Avoidance: the dance around avoiding the void. Avoiding what we do not know how to do, or be with in a different way.

Autism: a developmental disability affecting empathy, communication, and socialization.

Autonomic nervous system: part of the nervous system that regulates organ function, metabolism, and homeostasis.

Awareness: conscious recognition and direct knowing.

Axis mundi: a fulcrum or alignment connecting the cosmos and the world, heaven and earth. The monopole.

Ballon: a ballet term describing lightness and ease in jumping. The dancer appears to pause in the air before descending, only to rebound and be suspended in the air again.

Barometer: an instrument used to measure air pressure and predict changes in the weather; something that is used to indicate or predict something.

Being: our larger intelligence; the essential love that we intrinsically are.

Central nervous system: the brain and spinal cord.

Chakra: a Sanskrit word meaning "wheel" or "disk." In yoga, meditation, and Ayurveda systems, chakras are described as wheels of energy throughout the body. There are seven main chakras, located in the body from the base of the spine to the crown of the head.

Citadel: any strongly fortified place; historically, a fortress or castle that commands a city.

Coalesce: to grow together or into one body; to unite so as to form one mass, community, or whole; to blend or come together.

Conduit: a pipe, tube, or the like for conveying water or other fluid; a similar natural passage.

Confidence: confiding-in-essence; connected with a larger truth; when my will surrenders to Thy will.

Continuum: a continuous series or whole, no part of which is perceptibly different from the adjacent parts.

Conundrum: a puzzling question or problem; a riddle.

Cranial sacral therapy: a relative of osteopathic therapy that stimulates innate healing. By using gentle hand pressure to manipulate the skeleton and connective tissues, the practitioner initiates reciprocal, rhythmic impulses that travel throughout the body, especially in the cerebrospinal fluid between the skull and the sacrum.

Crown chakra: the seventh chakra, located at the top of the head. It is the spiritual connection to our higher selves, the way to enlightenment, the path of Divine energy that is the Source of everything.

Crystalline: clear, transparent; pertaining to crystals and their ability to aid in receiving and sending communication.

Cuneiform: wedge-shaped characters used in Sumerian writing.

Decipher: to discover the meaning of anything obscure or difficult; to trace or understand.

Deficiency: a state of feeling deficient because of lack, incompleteness, or inability; insufficient capacity.

Discern: to distinguish or discriminate. To perceive by one's sight or some other sense (or by the intellect) to clearly see, recognize, or apprehend.

Dispensable: not necessary or essential; unworthy.

Dissociation: the state of being separate or disconnected from the whole. In psychiatry, this occurs when a group of mental processes split off from the main body of one's consciousness.

Distortion: to twist out of shape; make crooked or deformed; to give a false or perverted meaning; to misrepresent.

Dowser: water finder; a divining rod; a person skilled in the rod's use (also see, "witching for waters").

Effulgent: shining forth brilliantly, fully radiant.

Ego: a self-identity formulated upon the beliefs created around coping. Out of a sense of separation from the whole, one forms the concept of an ego.

Egoic/egoistic: of or relating to the ego.

Embodiment: the practical cultivation of being grounded in the body along with expansive perceptual awareness at the same time.

Eminence: a high place or part, a hill or elevation; a high station, rank, or repute.

Empirical: derived from or guided by experience or experiment; depending upon experience or observation alone, without using scientific method or theory.

Grand battement: a ballet term; throwing the working leg high in the air and coming back down to position.

En masse: in a mass; all together; connected as a group.

Entrained: a phenomenon of the body in which its autonomic mechanism synchs up with strong, external rhythms, pulses, or beats.

Epinoia: spirit of the Light within.

Equanimity: mental or emotional stability or composure, especially under tension or strain; calmness; equilibrium, fairness, impartiality.

Esoteric: specialized, subtle obscure knowledge intended for enlightenment.

Espouse: to adopt or give support to a cause, an ideal, and so forth.

Essence: the virtuous nature of the innate love of one's soul.

Fibromyalgia: a condition of widespread musculoskeletal pain accompanied by fatigue, sleep, memory, and mood issues. Such conditions amplify pain by affecting how the brain processes pain signals.

Flagellating: the act of whipping, scourging, flogging, or lashing oneself. Self-inflicted pain.

Fulcrum: the point from which an entire system is able to remain balanced.

Geomancer: someone who discovers hidden knowledge with the aid of signs, symbols, and supernatural power; interpreting the pattern of the land.

Grokked: understood thoroughly and intuitively.

Groundedness: a state of being firm, solid, sensible, and down-to-earth; having one's feet on the ground.

Groundlessness: baseless, without ground, ungrounded.

Gustatory: the sensation of tasting.

Helix: a three-dimensional shape winding uniformly around a spiral.

Hypervigilance: an extreme state of being watchful and on guard to detect danger; extremely wary, awake, and alert.

Imaginal: the absolute emptiness out of which everything is formed. The essential relationship between spirit and matter.

Imminent: likely to occur at any moment; impending.

Inadequacy: the state of being not sufficient or enough; inept, unsuitable, or defective.

Incongruence: inconsistent, conflicting messages; incomplete, incompatible, discordant that negatively affect other parts.

Incriminate: to accuse, implicate, or charge with responsibility for all or part of a negative outcome.

Ineffable: inexpressible; not to be spoken because of its sacredness; unutterable.

Innate: native; inherent in the essential character of something.

Innumerable: beyond what can be counted; countless.

Inoculations: the introduction of a principle into a medium to cause growth and multiplication.

Instantaneous: occurring at once, or completed in an instant.

Insula: area of the brain that is key in mapping emotional awareness, empathy, and physiological self-regulation.

Integrity: being whole; unified; sound ethical character; honesty.

Integral: relating to or belonging as a part of the whole; necessary to the completeness of the whole.

Intuitive: direct perception of truth or fact independent of any reasoning process.

Intuition cells: Von Economo cells found in brains of advanced mammals. These cells allow fast, intuitive judgment and insight.

In utero: in the uterus or womb; unborn.

Juncture: something by which two things are joined; a point of time, especially one made critical or important by a concurrence of circumstances.

Kundalini: from Sanskrit; in the yogic tradition, a force of primal, subtle energy located at the base of the spine.

Lateral ventricals: brain structures that contain and drive cerebrospinal fluid, helping to circulate nutrients and remove waste.

Latifa: from Persian and Arabic: the subtle energy centers pertaining to the virtuous codes of the soul.

Matrix: a form or environment that constitutes the place or condition out of which something else originates, takes form, or develops.

Melatonin: a brain hormone made by the pineal gland that helps control sleep cycles.

Mirror neurons: intuition cells within high-level body maps that instantly read intentions and empathy; key to many higher mental functions.

Monatomic: having one atom in a molecule.

Monogamous: the condition of having only one mate; the practice of being married to only one person at a time.

Narcissistic: self-obsessed fascination with oneself; vain.

Obscuration: the act or state of being not clear, ambiguous, vague, or uncertain.

Orgon reflex: from the work of Wilhelm Reich: orgasmic-cosmic energy when unimpeded naturally flows through the body.

Ortho-bionomy: a gentle, noninvasive, osteopathically-based form of physical and energetic body therapy.

Osteopathic: medicine in which doctors use their hands to diagnose illness and injury to encourage the body's natural tendency toward self-healing.

Overwhelm: the flooding of emotions, sensations, and thoughts; too much, too soon, too fast.

Paradigm: a philosophical or theoretical framework of any kind; an outstandingly clear example or archetype.

Parasympathetic nervous system: regulates digestion, rest, elimination, and calming of the emotions and body.

Pendulate: to swing back and forth between opposite poles from a fixed point.

Peripersonal space: the field or space around the body that the brain includes in its body map.

Periphery: an area lying beyond the strict limits of a thing.

Phenomenon: rare or significant event; an exceptional, unusual, person, thing, occurrence, or aspect known through the senses rather than by thought or intuition.

Phenomenological: the study of the development of human consciousness and self-awareness; a philosophical movement that describes the structure of the objects of awareness and of awareness itself in abstraction from any claims concerning existence.

Piezoluminescence: light emission induced in certain solids by nondestructive dynamic pressure.

Pineal gland: meaning "face of God"; a small, conical appendage with the essential structure of an eye; an endocrine gland in the brain that produces melatonin and maintains circadian rhythm.

Pituitary axis: the hypothalamic–pituitary–adrenal axis is a complex set of direct influences and feedback interactions among three endocrine glands. A major neuroendocrine system that controls reactions to stress and regulates many body processes.

Presencing: the act of being present in an unbiased manner with arising sensation and thoughts; being with.

Proprioception: an internal sense of awareness and feedback of how and where the body and parts of the body are oriented in space.

Psychoactive: affecting mind or behavior.

Psycho-spiritual: an approach to healing using psychological theories of human growth and a spiritual approach to recognizing and accessing higher consciousness.

PTSD: Posttraumatic stress disorder; a condition triggered by one or more overwhelming events. Symptoms may include flashbacks, nightmares, severe anxiety, and uncontrollable thoughts about the event.

Quantum: a discrete quantity of energy proportional in magnitude to the frequency of the radiation it represents.

Reality: real-i-tied; the nature of True Self; the state of things as they exist. Seeing things as they are.

Re-sourcing: a source of supply or support; an available means that enhances the quality of life.

Revelations: acts of revealing in order to view or make known; enlightening or astonishing disclosures.

Ridwan School of Enlightenment/ The Diamond Approach/ The Diamondlogos Teachings: contemporary teachings that developed within the context of both ancient spiritual teachings and modern depth psychology theory.

Sabotage: to deliberately destroy, hurt or undermine.

Self-actualization: healthy individuation and expression of True Self.

Self-realization: the reality and direct experiential knowing of True Self.

Sentient: feeling emotions or sensing physical sensations.

Seraphim: an order of 6-winged angels continuously praising God.

Serendipitous: beneficial discoveries made as if by accident.

Serotonin: a neurotransmitter that carries signals along the nerve cells, promoting balance in the body and regulating mood and well-being.

Shamanism: an ancient divination and healing practice connecting to nature and all of creation; a system of accessing and influencing the world of spirits.

Shamballa: a place of peace, tranquility, and happiness; paradise.

Somatic: relating to the physical body and sensations.

Source: a generative force; a point of origin; Creation.

Spiritual narcissism: an inflated ego defense disguised as being spiritually superior.

Subtle: delicate, elusive, hidden, obscure, difficult to understand or perceive.

Subtleties: qualities or states of being subtle.

Sufi: one who practices a contemplative mystical process of self-transformation; directly receiving experience of and from the divine.

Sufic: of or about the Sufi practice and experience.

Sufism: a hidden, esoteric wisdom-dimension that underlies the sacred heart transmission of all religions, dating back through the early Gnostic mystics, to the Essenes, the ancient Pythagorean orders, the mystery schools of the Egyptians and Zoroastrians, Kabbalists, and Islamic Sufi sects. A nondual practice uniting with the One that unites us all.

Sumerian: the language of, or a native of, Sumer, which is part of ancient Babylonia.

Sympathetic nervous system: the involuntary arousal response of fight, flight, freeze, or appease.

Synapse: the point at which some nervous impulse passes from one neuron to anther.

Synergy: a mutually advantageous compatibility that results when two or more work together.

Telepathic: having the ability to know another person's thoughts without being told what they are; able to read minds.

Teleport: to transport or be transported across space and distance instantly.

Terrain: the particular features of a land or area.

Thwart: to prevent a successful outcome.

Titration: the process of adding measured amounts of a substance to a known volume until a desired end point is reached.

Transmute: to completely change the form, appearance, or nature of someone or something.

True Self: direct illuminated self-knowledge and embodiment of self as Source.

Undulating: the act of moving like waves.

Upanishads: from Sanskrit: a collection of religious and philosophical texts written in India (c. 800 BCE–c. 500 BCE) by saints and seers of their first-hand accounts of God.

Vacuous: lacking content that could or should be present; vacant, empty, void.

Velocity: high rate of movement; swiftness.

Ventricles: two sections in the heart that pump blood to the body; areas in the brain that exchange cerebrospinal fluid.

Witching for water: also known as "water dowsing." This is the practice of using a forked stick, rod, pendulum, or similar device to locate underground water, minerals, or other hidden or lost substances.

Witnessing: the ability to clearly see, hear, or feel firsthand an objective, truthful account of what is happening.

Chapter Notes

Chapter 1

1. Omar Khayyam, "Quatrain 88," *Rubaiyat of Omar Khayyam*, translated by Edward FitzGerald {Garden City, NY: Garden City Books, 1952}. Retrieved from: http//www.lieder.net/lieder/get text.html Text Id=3548

2. Wali Ali Meyer, Bilal Hyde, Faisal Muqaddam, and Shabda Kahn, *Physicians of the Heart: A Sufi View of the Ninety-Nine Names of Allah* {San Francisco, CA: Sufi Ruhaniat International, 2011} pp. 21, 22

3. Henry Bayman, *The Station of No Station: Open Secrets of the Sufis* {Berkeley, CA: North Atlantic Press, 2001} p. 143

4. A. H. Almaas, *The Point of Existence: Transformations of Narcissism in Self-Realization* {Berkeley, CA: Diamond Books, 1996} pp. 21, 22

5. Hugh Milne, *The Heart of Listening 1: A Visionary Approach to Craniosacral Work* {Berkeley, CA: North Atlantic Books, 1995} pp. 152, 153

6. Tarthang Tulku, *Dynamics of Time and Space: Transcending Limits of Knowledge* {Berkeley, CA: Dharma Publishing, 1994} pp. 73-78

Chapter 2

1. The Thunder, *Perfect Mind* {NHC V1, 2} {CG VI.2:13,1-21,32} pp. 14, 33-34. Translation copyright Ann McGuire, 2000 http://www.stoa.org/diotima/anthology/thunder.shtml

2. Hazrat Inayat Khan, *The Soul's Journey* {New York, NY: Omega Publications, 1707/2003} pp. 34, 263, 264

3. Pir Vilayat Inayat Khan, *The Ecstasy Beyond Knowing: A Manual of Meditation* {New Lebanon, NY: Omega Publications, 1841/2014} pp. 251, 252

4. Hazrat Inayat Khan, *Spiritual Dimensions of Psychology* {New Lebanon, NY: Omega Publications, 1981} pp. 243-245

5. A. H. Almaas, *The Pearl Beyond Price: Integration of Personality Into Being {An Object Relations Approach}* {Berkeley, CA: Diamond Books, 1988} pp. 375-377

6. Alexander Lowen, *Bioenergetics* {New York, NY: Penguin Compass, 1975} pp. 142-145

7. Sandra Blakeslee and Mathew Blakeslee, *The Body Has a Mind of Its Own: How Body Maps in Your Brain Help You Do {Almost} Everything Better* {New York, NY, Random House, 2007} p. 190

8. Wali Ali Meyer, Bilal Hyde, Faisal Muqaddam, and Shabda Kahn, *Physicians of the Heart: A Sufi View of the Ninety-Nine Names of Allah* {San Francisco, CA: Sufi Ruhaniat International, 2011} pp. 53, 95, 96

Chapter 3

1. Kabir, "Within This Body," in *Perfume of the Desert: Inspirations From Sufi Wisdom*, translated by Andrew Harvey and Eryk Hanut {Wheaton, IL: Quest Books, c.1999} p. 46. Published by permission.

2. "Maktubat Imam-i-Rabbani," *Ma'arif-i-Ladunniyya*, by Imam Rabbani Mujaddid Alf-e-Sani Shaykh Ahmad Sirhindi Faruqi (d. 1034 AH). Translator, Sayyid Zawwar Hussain Shah Naqshbandi (d. 1984). Published by Zawwar Academy Publications, Karachi, 2012 (first published 1969). Digitized by Maktabah Mujaddidiyah (www.maktabah.org) May 2012. Retrieved from: http://love-real.com/english-translation-maktubat-imam-rabbani/100.php, p. 7

3. Franklyn Sills, *Craniosacral Biodynamics: Volume 1, The Breath of Life, Biodynamics, and Fundamental Skills* {Berkeley, CA: North Atlantic Books, 2001} p. 62

4. John Upledger and Jon D. Vredevoogd, *Craniosacral Therapy* {Seattle, WA: Eastland Press, 1983} p. 645. Gerald Clark, *The Anunnaki of Nibiru: Mankind's Forgotten Creators, Enslavers, Saviors, and Hidden Architects of the New World Order* {Gerald Clark/CreateSpace, 2013} pp. 13, 14, 41, 42, 91, 100, 103

6. Jeremy Narby, *The Cosmic Serpent: DNA and the Origins of Knowledge* {New York, NY: Jeremy F. Tarcher/Putnam, 1998} pp. 65, 86-88

7. Gregg Braden, *The God Code: The Secret of Our Past, the Promise of Our Future* {Carlsbad, CA: Hay House, 2004} pp. 137-140

8. David Wilcock, *The Source Field Investigations: The Hidden Science and Lost Civilizations Behind the 2012 Prophecies* {New York, NY: Plume, 2011} pp. 55-63 (ch 2, nn. 2,3)

9. See: http://articles.mercola.com/sites/articles/archive/2013/04/30/water-flouridation-facts.aspx

10. Henry Corbin, *The Man of Light in Iranian Sufism* {New York, NY: Omega Publications, 1971} pp. 43-46, 70. Retrieved from: http://www.academia.edu/1268417/Between_Heidegger_and_the_Hidden_Imam_Reflections_on_Henry_Corbins_Approaches_to_Mystical_Islam111. Pir Vilayat Inayat Khan, *The Ecstasy Beyond Knowing: A Manual of Meditation* {New Lebanon, NY: Omega Publications, 1841/2014} pp. 290-292

Chapter 4

1. *The Secret Book of John: The Gnostic Gospel—Annotated and Explained,* translation and annotation by Stevan Davis {Woodstock, VT: Sky-light Paths Publishing, 2015} p. 111

2. David Abram, *The Spell of the Sensuous* {New York, NY: Vintage Books, 1996} pp. 59-61

3. William C. Chittick, *Imaginal Worlds* {Albany, NY: State University of New York Press, 1994} pp. 74-79

4. S. Radhakrishnan, *The Principal Upanishads* {New York, NY: HarperCollins Publishers, 2014} pp. 202, 203

5. Gregg Braden, *The Divine Matrix: Bridging Time, Space, Miracles, and Belief* {New York, NY: Hay House, 2007} p. 13

Chapter 5

1. Sogal Rimpoche, *The Tibetan Book of Living and Dying* {Revised and Updated}, edited by Patrick Gaffney and Andrew Harvey {San Francisco, CA: Rigpa Fellowship/HarperCollins, 2002], p. 40. Reprinted by permission of HarperCollins Publishers.

2. Canale, S., "Acute Traumatic Lesions of Ligaments," *Campbell's Operative Orthopedics* {ninth edition} {St. Louis, MO: Mosby} p. 1154

3. Diane Poole Heller and Laurence S. Heller, *Crash Course: A Self-Healing Guide to Auto Accident Trauma and Recovery* {Berkeley, CA: North Atlantic Books, 2001} pp. 36-38, 76

4. Hannah B. Harvey, The Art of Storytelling: From Parents to Professionals {Chantilly, VA: The Great Courses, 2013} pp. 5, 6

5. Peter A. Levine with Ann Frederick, *Waking the Tiger: Healing Trauma* {Berkeley, CA: North Atlantic Books, 2001} pp. 3, 12, 20, 21, 265, 266

Chapter 6

1. Oscar Wilde, Freire Wright, and Michael Foreman, *The Nightingale and the Rose* {London: Kaye & Ward, 1981}

2. Laurence Heller and Aline La Pierre, *Healing Developmental Trauma: How Early Trauma Affects Self-Regulation, Self-Image, and the Capacity for Relationship* {Berkeley, CA: North Atlantic Books, 2012} pp. 138-140, 215

3. Satprem, *The Mind of the Cells, or Willed Mutation of Our Species* {New York, NY: Institute for Evolutionary Research, 1982} pp. 134, 135

4. Glenn R. Schiraldi, *The Post-Traumatic Stress Disorder Sourcebook* {New York, NY: McGraw-Hill, 1947, 2000} pp. 30-33

5. Peter A. Levine with Ann Frederick, *"Waking the Tiger: Healing Trauma* {Berkeley, CA: North Atlantic Books, 1997} pp. 28, 32, 137, 164, 165, 157

Chapter 7

1. "Katha-Upanishad: 10, Sixth Aalli," *The Upanishad, Part 2* {SBE 15}, translated by Max Muller {1879} 23. Retrieved from: www: sacred-texts.com {Sacred Books of the East, Volume 15, 1879}, Kindle edition published by Evinity, Inc., 2009
2. A. H. Almaas, *The Pearl Beyond Price: Integration of Personality Into Being: An Object Relations Approach* {Berkeley, CA: Diamond Books, 1988} pp. 294, 295, 383-385, 388, 398, 399
3. Wali Ali Meyer, Bilal Hyde, Faisal Muqaddam, and Shabda Kahn, *Physicians of the Heart: A Sufi View of the Ninety-Nine Names of Allah* {San Francisco, CA: Sufi Ruhaniat International, 2011} pp. 94-99
4. Peter A. Levine, *Trauma and Memory: Brain and Body in a Search for the Living Past* {Berkeley, CA: North Atlantic Books, 2015} pp. 42-50, 53, 55, 63-71
5. Bessel Van Der Kolk, *The Body Keeps Score: Brain, Mind, and Body in the Healing of Trauma* {New York, NY: Penguin Books, 2014} p. 240

Chapter 8

1. *The Holy Qur'an* (fourth edition), text, translation, and commentary by Abdullah Yusuf Ali {Elmhurst, NY: Thahrike Tarsile Qur'an, Inc., 2002} Sura LXXVIII 1-7, p. 1719
2. Henry Corbin, *The Man of Light in Iranian Sufism* {New York, NY: Omega Publications Inc., 1971} pp. 31-35, 105
3. A. H. Almaas, *The Point of Existence: Transformations of Narcissism in Self-Realization* {Berkeley, CA: Diamond Books, 1996} p. 442

4. Peter A. Levine, *Trauma and Memory: Brain and Body in a Search for the Living Past* {Berkeley, CA: North Atlantic Books, 2015} pp. 131-133
5. Bessel Van Der Kolk, *The Body Keeps Score: Brain, Mind, and Body in the Healing of Trauma* {New York, NY: Penguin Books, 2014} pp. 109, 209, 356
6. Cass Ingram, *The Body Shape Diet* {Vernon Hills, IL, 2009} pp. 118-121

Chapter 9

1. Tarik Muqaddam, "Opposites" {Richmond, CA, 1993}. Used with permission.
2. Robert Maurer and Michelle Gifford, Mastering Fear: Harness Emotion to Achieve Excellence in Health, Work and Relationships {Wayne, NJ: The Career Press, 2016}
3. Michael Talbot, *The Holographic Universe* {New York, NY: HarperCollins Publishers, 1991} pp. 139-143
4. Henry Corbin, *The Man of Light in Iranian Sufism* {New York, NY: Omega Publications Inc., 1994} pp. 99, 101, 108
5. Gregg Braden, *The Divine Matrix: Bridging Time, Space, Miracles, and Belief* {Carlsbad, CA: Hay House, 2007} pp. 109, 110 pp. 158-160
6. Hazel Gilley, "Truth" {Lacey, WA, 2015}. Used with permission.

Chapter 10

1. Daniel Ladinsky, "It's Rigged," *Love Poems From God: Twelve Sacred Voices From the East and West* {New York, NY: Penguin Compass, 2002} page. Used with permission.

2. Judith Voirst, *Necessary Losses*, {New York, NY: The Free Press, 2002} pp. 48, 49, 57-61

3. Joseph Murphy, *The Power of Your Subconscious Mind* {New York, NY: Prentice Hall Press, 2008} pp. 109, 238-241

4. Laurence Heller and Aline La Pierre, *Healing Developmental Trauma: How Early Trauma Affects Self-Regulation, Self-Image, and the Capacity for Relationship* {Berkeley, CA: North Atlantic Books, 2012} pp. 108, 109

5. Thomas Bahler, *What You Want Wants You* {Aesop Publishing, 2014} pp. 75, 56

6. Wali Ali Meyer, Bilal Hyde, Faisal Muqaddam, and Shabda Kahn, *Physicians of the Heart: A Sufi View of the Ninety-Nine Names of Allah* {San Francisco, CA: Sufi Ruhaniat International, 2011} pp. 283-296

7. Hazrat Inayat Khan, *The Inner Life* {Boston, MA: Shamballa, 1997} pp. 16-20

Chapter 11

1. Daniel Ladinsky, "Wild Forces," *Love Poems From God: Twelve Sacred Voices From the East and West* {2002}, p. 47. Used with permission.

2. Joanne Cooper, "Cows" {poem}, {Carlton, WA, 2015}. Used with permission.

3. Estelle Frankel, *Sacred Therapy: Jewish Spiritual Teachings on Emotional Healing and Inner Wholeness* {Boston, MA: Shamballa, 2003} pp. 58-61

4. Gregg Braden, *The Divine Matrix: Bridging Time, Space, Miracles, and Belief* {Carlsbad, CA: Hay House, Inc.: 2007} pp. xvi xxii

5. Wali Ali Meyer, Bilal Hyde, Faisal Muqaddam, and Shabda Kahn, *Physicians of the Heart: A Sufi View of the Ninety-Nine*

Names of Allah {San Francisco, CA: Sufi Ruhaniat International, 2011} pp. 1, 106, 160-162, 203, 204

Chapter 12

1. Nan Shepard, *The Living Mountain* {Edinburgh and London, UK: Canongate, 2011} p. 108. Used with permission.
2. Satprem, *The Mind of the Cells, or Willed Mutation of Our Species* {Paris, France: Robert Laffont, S. A., 1981; New York, NY: Institute for Evolutionary Research, 1982} pp. 97-99
3. The Urantia Foundation, *The Urantia Book: A Revelation* {Chicago, IL: Urantia Foundation: 1955; New York, NY: Uversa Press, 1973} pp. 9, 10
4. Fran DiBiase, "In Love You Will Be Found" {Home, WA, 2016}. Used with permission.
5. Estelle Frankel, *Sacred Therapy: Jewish Spiritual Teachings on Emotional Healing and Inner Wholeness* {Boston, MA: Shamballa, 2003} pp. 63-68

Chapter 13

1. Cheri Dale {AKA Kim Lincoln}, "Star Light," *A Garden of Songs for the Magical Child* {CD} {www.CDBaby.com, 1995}
2. David Wilcock, *The Source Field Investigations: The Hidden Science and Lost Civilizations Behind the 2012 Prophecies* {New York, NY: Plume Book, 2011} pp. 460, 461
3. Peter A. Levine, *Trauma and Memory: Brain and Body in Search for the Living Past* {Berkeley, CA: North Atlantic Books, 2015} pp. 156-159
4. Annalee Skarin, *Secrets of Eternity* {Los Angeles, CA: De Vorss & Co. Publishers, 1960} pp. 229-235

5. Tarthang Tulku, *Dynamics of Time and Space: Transcending Limits on Knowledge* {Berkeley, CA: Dharma Publishing, 1994} pp. 61-63

Chapter 14

1. The Findhorn Community, *The Findhorn Garden Story* {Scotland, UK: The Findhorn Press, 1975/2008} p. 79. Used with permission.
2. Tarthang Tulku, *Dynamics of Time and Space: Transcending Limits on Knowledge* {Berkeley, CA.: Dharma Publishing, 1994} pp. 118-121
3. Lynne McTaggart, *The Field: The Quest for the Sacred Force of the Universe* {Great Britain: HarperCollins, 2001} pp. 121, 122
4. Joseph Murphy, *The Power of Your Subconscious Mind* {Reward Books, 2000. New York, NY: Prentice Hall Press, 2008} pp. 247-250
5. Wali Ali Meyer, Bilal Hyde, Faisal Muqaddam, and Shabda Kahn, *Physicians of the Heart: A Sufi View of the Ninety-Nine Names of Allah* {San Francisco, CA: Sufi Ruhaniat International, 2011} pp. 83-90

Chapter 15

1. Maktubat Imam Rabbini, Mujadd Alf sani, Sheikh Ahmed si-rhindi, *Ma'arif-i Ladunniyya* {Twenty-sixth Marifat}, English translation {6-First Volume, 99th letter}. Retrieved from www.love-real.com/english-translation-maktubat-imam-rabbani/7.php
2. Sandra Blakeslee and Matthew Blakeslee, *The Body Has a Mind of Its Own* {New York, NY: Random House, 2007} pp. 18, 121, 178, 187-189, 194-198

3. V. S. Ramachanran, "Autism Linked to Mirror Neuron Dysfunction," *Scientific American*, Nov. 1, 2006

4. Lynne McTaggart, *The Field: The Quest for the Sacred Force of the Universe* {New York, NY: HarperCollins, 2002} pp. 225, 226

Chapter 16

1. The Prophet Muhammed, "Prayer of Light," translated by Hazrat Pir Moineddin Jablonsky {short version}, {San Francisco, CA: Sufi Ruhaniat Society worldwide. Retrieved from http://www.ruhaniat.org/index.php/sri-locations#US

2. Juliet Lane, "Lists" {Olympia, WA, 2016}. Used with permission.

3. Heidi Jo, "We die so that we may live..." {Olympia, WA, 2016}. Used with permission.

Chapter 17

1. Hafiz, "There Are So Many Gifts," *The Gift: Poems by Hafiz the Great Sufi Master*, translated by Daniel Ladinsky {New York, NY: Penguin Compass, 1999}, pp. 67-68. Used with permission.

2. Samuel Aun Weor, *Alchemy and Kabbalah in the Tarot: The Keys for Radical Spiritual Transformation* {Brooklyn, NY: Glorian, 2012} pp. 144, 145

3. Pir Zia Inayat Khan, *Caravan of Souls* {New Lebanon, NY: Suluk Press, 2012} pp. 2, 3, 104-106, 124, 125

4. A. H. Almaas, *The Pearl Beyond Price: Integration of Personality Into Being {An Object Relations Approach}* {Berkeley, CA: Diamond Books, 1998} pp. 417-421

5. Henry Bayman, *The Station of No Station: Open Secrets of the Sufis* {Berkeley, CA: North Atlantic Books, 2001} pp. 199-202

Chapter 18

1. "The Poems of Abu Sa'id Abu'l Khwyr: Poet 967-1049" {Classic Persian Literature} by Reza Ordoubadian {*Friends of Silence Newsletter*, Feb. 2002} Vol. xv, No 1

2. L. Frank Baum, *The Wonderful Wizard of Oz* {New York, NY: Barnes & Noble Classics, 1900/2005}

3. Wali Ali Meyer, Bilal Hyde, Faisal Muqaddam, and Shabda Kahn, *Physicians of the Heart: A Sufi View of the Ninety-Nine Names of Allah* {San Francisco, CA: Sufi Ruhaniat International, 2011} pp. 1, 101, 203, 255

4. Hazrat Inayat Khan, *The Inner Life* {Boston, MA: Shambhala, 1997} pp. 66, 67, 69-76

5. A. H. Almaas, *The Pearl Beyond Price: Integration of Personality Into Being {An Object Relations Approach}* {Berkeley, CA: Diamond Books, 1998} pp. 100-108

6. Judith Viorst, *Necessary Losses* {New York, NY: The Free Press, 2002} pp. 41-50

7. Estelle Frankel, *Sacred Therapy: Jewish Spiritual Teachings on Emotional Healing and Inner Wholeness* {Boston, MA: Shambhala, 2003} pp. 128, 129

Chapter 19

1. Paramahansa Yogananda, "I would like to see..." in Daya Mata, "Paramahansa––As I Knew Him," *Self-Realization Magazine* {Los Angeles, CA: Self-Realization Fellowship, 1981} Fall. Used with permission.

2. Pir Zia Inayat Khan, *Caravan of Souls* {New Lebanon, NY: Suluk Press, 2012} pp. 124, 125

3. A. H. Almaas, *The Unfolding Now: Realizing Your True Nature Through the Practice of Presence* {Boston, MA: Shambhala, 2008} pp. 114-124

4. Rudolf Steiner, *A Way of Self-Knowledge: And the Threshold of the Spiritual World* {London: Rudolf Steiner Press, 1975; Hudson, NY: Anthroposophic Press, 1999} pp. xx, xxi

5. S. Radhikrishnan, *The Principal Upanishads* {First published in 1953 in Great Britain: Allen & Unwin Ltd.; New York, NY: HarperCollins, 2014} pp. 76, 78

6. A. H. Almaas, *The Pearl Beyond Price: Integration of Personality Into Being {An Object Relations Approach}* {Berkeley, CA: Diamond Books, 1988} pp. 475-481

7. Hazrat Inayat Khan, *The Inner Life* {Boston, MA: Shambhala, 1997} pp. 59-62

Chapter 20

1. Pir Zia Inayat Khan, "Murshid's Blessing," *Caravan of Souls: An Introduction to the Sufi Path of Hazrat Inayat Khan* {New Lebanon, NY: Suluk Press, 2013} p. 195. Used with permission.

2. Pir Vilayat Inayat Khan, *The Ecstasy Beyond Knowing: A Manual of Meditation* {New Lebanon, NY, 1993} pp. 77, 78

3. Henry Corbin, *Alone With the Alone: Creative Imagination in the Sufism of Ibn' Arabi* {Princeton, NJ: Princeton University Press, 1969} pp. 336, 337

4. 4. Janet M. Magiera, *Aramaic New Testament Translation* {LWM Publications, A Division

References

Abram, David. {1996}. *The Spell of the Sensuous*. New York, NY: Vintage Books.

Alf sani, Mujaddid. [n.d.]. English translation of Maktubat Imam-i-Rabbani. Retrieved from http://love-real.com/english-translation-maktubat-imam-rabbani/14.php

Ali, Abdullah Yusuf. {2002}. *The Holy Qur'an*. New York, NY: Thahrik Tarsile, Inc. Publishers.

Almaas, A. H. {1988}. *The Pearl Beyond Price: Integration of Personality Into Being, An Object Relations Approach*. Berkeley, CA: Diamond Books.

Almaas, A. H. {1996}. *The Point of Existence*. Berkeley, CA: Diamond Books.

Almaas, A. H. {2008}. *The Unfolding Now*. Boston, MA: Shambala.

Bayman, Henry. {2001}. *The Station of No Station: Open Secrets of the Sufis.*

Berkeley, CA: North Atlantic Books.

Bahler, Thomas. {2014}. *What You Want Wants You.* Aesop Publishing.

Blakeslee, Sandra, and Blakeslee, Mathew. {2007}. *The Body Has a Mind of Its Own.* New York, NY: Random House.

Braden, Gregg {2007}. *The Divine Matrix: Bridging Time, Space, Miracles, and Belief.* Carlsbad, CA: Hay House.

Canale, S. {1998}. *Campbell's Orthopedics: Acute Traumatic Lesions of Ligaments.* St. Louis, MO: Elsevier Health Bookshop.

Chittick, William C. {1994}. *Imaginal Worlds.* Albany, NY: State of New York Press.

Clark, Gerald, MSEE PSI. {2013}. *The Anunnaki of Nibiru.* Gerald Clark.

Cohen, Leonard. {n.d.}. "Anthem" {lyrics}. Retrieved from http://www.songlyrics.com/leonard-cohen/anthem-lyrics/

Corbin, Henry. {1969}. *Alone With the Alone.* Princeton, NJ: Princeton University Press.

Corbin, Henry. {1971}. *The Man of Light.* New York, NY: Omega Publications.

Dale, Cheri. {1995}. *A Garden of Songs for the Magical Child.* Portland, OR: CDBaby.com

Davis, Steven. {2005}. *The Secret Book of John: The Gnostic Gospel Annotated and Explained*. Woodstock, VT: Sky-light Paths Publishing.

Frankel, Estelle. {2003}. *Sacred Therapy: Jewish Spiritual Teachings on Emotional Healing*. Boston, MA: Shamballa.

Findhorn Community. {1975}. *The Findhorn Garden*. Scotland, UK: Findhorn Press.

Harvey, Andrew, and Hanut, Eryk. {1999}. *Perfume of the Desert*. Wheaton, IL: Quest Books.

Harvey, Hannah B. {2013}. *The Art of Storytelling: From Parents to Professionals*. Chantilly, VA: The Great Courses.

Heller, Laurence, and LaPierre, Aline. {2012}. *Healing Developmental Trauma*. Berkeley, CA: North Atlantic Books.

Ingram, Cass. {2009}. *The Body Shape Diet*. Vernon Hills, IL: Knowledge House Publishers.

Khan, Hazrat Inayat. {1997}. *The Inner Life*. Boston, MA: Shamballa.

Khan, Hazrat Inayat. {2003}. *The Soul's Journey*. New York, NY: Omega Publications.

Khan, Hazrat Inayat. {1981}. *Spiritual Dimensions of Psychology*. New York, NY: Omega Publications.

Khan, Pir Vilayat Inayat. {2007}. *The Ecstasy Beyond Knowing*. New York, NY: Suluk Press.

Khayyam, Omar. {1959}. "Quattrain 88," *Rubaiyat*. Translated by Edward Fitzgerald. Retrieved from http://lieder.net

Ladinsky, Daniel. {2002}. *Love Poems From God: Twelve Sacred Voices of the East and West*. New York, NY: Penguin Compass.

Larson, William J. {1993}. *Human Embryology*. New York, NY: Churchill Livingston.

Levine, Peter A., with Frederick, Ann. {1997}. *Waking the Tiger*. Berkeley, CA: North Atlantic Books.

Levine, Peter A. {2015}. *Trauma and Memory: Brain and Body in a Search for the Living Past*. Berkeley, CA: North Atlantic Books.

Lowen, Alexander. {1975}. *Bioenergetics*. New York, NY: Penguin Compass.

Meyer, Wali Ali, Hyde, Bilal, Muqaddam, Faisal, and Kahn, Shabda. {2011}. *Physicians of the Heart*. San Francisco, CA: Sufi Ruhaniat International.

Maurer, Robert, and Gifford, Michelle. {2016}. *Mastering Fear*. Wayne, NJ: Career Press.

Milne, Hugh. {1995}. *The Heart of Listening 1*. Berkeley, CA: North Atlantic Books.

McTaggart, Lynne. {2002}. *The Field: The Quest for the Secret Force of the Universe*. New York, NY: HarperCollins.

Murphy, Joseph. {n.d.}, revised by Ian McMahan, 2000}. *The Power of Your Subconscious Mind*. Reward Books.

Muller, Max. {1879}. *The Upanishads, Part 2* {SBE 15}. Retrieved from www.sacred-texts.com

Narby, Jeremy. {1998}. *The Cosmic Serpent*, New York: Jeremy F. Tarcher/ Putman

Poole Heller, Diane, and Heller, Laurence. {2001}. *Crash Course: A Self-Healing Guide to Accident Trauma and Recovery*. Berkeley, CA: North Atlantic Books.

Radhakrishnan, S. {1953} *The Principal Upanishads*. London, Great Britain: Allen & Unwin Ltd.

Satprem. {1982}. *The Mind of the Cells*. New York, NY: Institute for Evolutionary Research.

Schiraldi, Glenn R. {2000}. *The Post-Traumatic Stress Disorder Workbook*. New York, NY: McGraw-Hill.

Sills, Franklin. {2001}. *Craniosacral Biodynamics, Vol 1*. Berkeley, CA: North Atlantic Books.

Shepherd, Nan. {2011}. *The Living Mountain*. London, UK: Canongate.

Skarin, Annalee. {1960}. *Secrets of Eternity*. Los Angeles, CA: DeVorss & Co. Publishers.

Sogal Rimpoche. {2002} *The Tibetan Book of Living and Dying*. New York, NY: HarperCollins.

Steiner, Rudolf. {1969}. *A Way of Self-Knowledge*: A*nd the Threshold of the Spiritual World*. New York, NY: Anthroposophic Press.

Talbot, Michael. {1991}. *The Holographic Universe*. New York, NY: HarperCollins.

Thunder, The. {n.d.}. *Perfect Mind* {350 CE}. Coptic version found at Nag Hammadi. Retrieved from http://gnosis.org/naghamm/thunder. html

Tulku, Tarthang. {1994}. *Dynamics of Time and Space*. Berkeley, CA: Dharma Publishing.

Van Der Kolk, Bessel A. {2014}. *The Body Keeps Score*. New York, NY: Penguin.

Viorst, Judith. {2002}. *Necessary Losses*. New York, NY: The Free Press.

Wilcock, David. {2011}. *The Source Field Investigations: The Hidden Science and Lost Civiliations Behind the 2012 Prophecies*. New York, NY: Plume.

Wilde, Oscar. {1981}. *The Rose and the Nightingale*. London, UK: Kaye & Ward.

About the Author

Kim Lincoln, the founder of the Terrain of Essence Teaching, has helped thousands of students on their paths to self-realization and somatic integration.

For over forty years, Lincoln has used a combination of energetic science and ancient mysticism to deliver workshops, guest presentations, and online classes. Her goal is to help individuals awaken so humanity can recognize itself as an interspecies collective and experience beneficial evolutionary change.

For further information about the school and training:
www.TerrainOfEssenceTeachings.com

To view tutorial videos or audios supporting exercises in this book:
www.KimLincoln.com/video

To arrange for a lecture or workshop in your area inquire:
info@KimLincoln.com

Learn about upcoming books and events by subscribing to our
newsletter (at the foot of either website)..

To purchase the channeled CD "A Garden of
Songs: For the Magical Child Within,"
send $15.00 {postage included} to:
Terrain of Essence
6227 Northill Dr. SW
Olympia, WA 98512